The
Irish
Americans

Other books in the Immigrants in America series:

The
Irish
Americans

By Karen Price Hossell

LUCENT
BOOKS®

THOMSON

GALE

San Diego • Detroit • New York • San Francisco • Cleveland • New Haven, Conn. • Waterville, Maine • London • Munich

On Cover: Irish Americans celebrate St. Patrick's Day in Boston.

© 2003 by Lucent Books. Lucent Books is an imprint of The Gale Group, Inc., a division of Thomson Learning, Inc.

Lucent Books® and Thomson Learning™ are trademarks used herein under license.

For more information, contact
Lucent Books
27500 Drake Rd.
Farmington Hills, MI 48331-3535
Or you can visit our Internet site at http://www.gale.com

Library of Congress Cataloging-in-Publication Data

Price Hossell, Karen, 1957–
    The Irish Americans / by Karen Price Hossell.
    p. cm. — (Immigrants in America)
Summary: Reviews the reasons why millions of Irish have immigrated to America, what their passage was like, the kind of jobs most found, communities they formed, and the discrimination they faced.
Includes bibliographical references and index.
    ISBN 1-56006-752-7 (hardback : alk. paper)
    1. Irish Americans—History—Juvenile literature. 2. Irish Americans—Social Conditions—Juvenile literature. 3. Immigrants—United States—History—Juvenile literature. 4. Ireland—Emigration and immigration—History—Juvenile literature. 5. United States—Emigration and immigration—History—Juvenile literature
[1. Irish Americans. 2. Immigrants. 3. United States—Emigration and immigration. 4. Ireland—Emigration and immigration.] I. Title. II. Series
    E184.I6P74 2003
    973'.049162—dc21

                                                                2002008117

CONTENTS

FOREWORD

Immigrants have come to America at different times, for different reasons, and from many different places. They leave their homelands to escape religious and political persecution, poverty, war, famine, and countless other hardships. The journey is rarely easy. Sometimes, it entails a long and hazardous ocean voyage. Other times, it follows a circuitous route through refugee camps and foreign countries. At the turn of the twentieth century, for instance, Italian peasants, fleeing poverty, boarded steamships bound for New York, Boston, and other eastern seaports. And during the 1970s and 1980s, Vietnamese men, women, and children, victims of a devastating war, began arriving at refugee camps in Arkansas, Pennsylvania, Florida, and California, en route to establishing new lives in the United States.

Whatever the circumstances surrounding their departure, the immigrants' journey is always made more difficult by the knowledge that they leave behind family, friends, and a familiar way of life. Despite this, immigrants continue to come to America because, for many, the United States represents something they could not find at home: freedom and opportunity for themselves and their children.

No matter what their reasons for emigrating, where they have come from, or when they left, once here, nearly all immigrants face considerable challenges in adapting and making the United States

their new home. Language barriers, unfamiliar surroundings, and sometimes hostile neighbors make it difficult for immigrants to assimilate into American society. Some Vietnamese, for instance, could not read or write in their native tongue when they arrived in the United States. This heightened their struggle to communicate with employers who demanded they be literate in English, a language vastly different from their own. Likewise, Irish immigrant school children in Boston faced classmates who teased and belittled their lilting accent. Immigrants from Russia often felt isolated, having settled in areas of the United States where they had no access to traditional Russian foods. Similarly, Italian families, used to certain wines and spices, rarely shopped or traveled outside of New York's Little Italy, a self-contained community cut off from the rest of the city.

Even when first-generation immigrants do successfully settle into life in the United States, their children, born in America, often have different values and are influenced more by their country of birth than their parents' traditions. Children want to be a part of the American culture and usually welcome American ideals, beliefs, and styles. As they become more Americanized—adopting western dating habits and fashions, for instance—they tend to cast aside or even actively reject the traditions embraced by their parents.

Assimilation, then, often becomes an ideological dispute that creates conflict among immigrants of every ethnicity. Whether Chinese, Italian, Russian, or Vietnamese, young people battle their elders for respect, individuality, and freedom, issues that often would not have come up in their homeland. And no matter how tightly the first generations hold onto their traditions, in the end, it is usually the young people who decide what to keep and what to discard.

The Immigrants in America series fully examines the immigrant experience. Each book in the series discusses why the immigrants left their homeland, what the journey to America was like, what they experienced when they arrived, and the challenges of assimilation. Each volume includes discussion of triumph and tragedy, contributions and influences, history and the future. Fully documented primary and secondary source quotations enliven the text. Sidebars highlight interesting events and personalities. Annotated bibliographies offer ideas for additional research. Each book in this dynamic series provides students with a wealth of information as well as launching points for further discussion.

From Desperation to Assimilation

The story of Irish Americans transcends superficialities like St. Patrick's Day, leprechauns, and lucky clover leaves. Instead, the story includes a battle against prejudice and poverty and their attendant hardships. Yet this is a story of triumph over these adversities. It is also a story that 44 million or so Americans today claim as their own.

Mere Survival

For most Irish Americans, the first chapters in their story are of difficulty and deprivation. Forced by starvation to leave their country, Irish famine immigrants, the largest group of Irish to arrive in the United States, came with little more than the clothes they carried in battered trunks. When they arrived they were generally anything but welcome. Usually, they were forced to disembark onto the streets of a foreign land. Far from finding easy riches, all they could hope for was a menial job that would pay enough to allow them to buy food and shelter. The newly arrived Irish had to use every means they knew just to survive.

As more Irish arrived in America, hope largely lay in sticking together and looking to one another for support. As the Irish settled in, Americans mostly welcomed them only for the cheap services and labor they provided. For their part, the Irish were happy to build an imaginary wall around themselves. As one writer notes, "Nothing about nineteenth-century America would change the Irish Catholic view of the outside world as a hostile, dangerous place to be kept at arm's length."[1] The Irish stayed in their own communities, venturing out to go to work, then returning home to the safety of their own.

Determination, Power, and Adaptability

Through patience and determination, Irish immigrants worked hard and made a place for themselves in America. Many first-generation immigrants died young—from exhaustion and illness in the years immediately following the famine—but they passed on to their children their determination; these young Irish Americans combined that determination with the opportunities the new land presented to make America their home.

Armed with determination, the children of famine immigrants worked not just to survive but to grasp the political power that would solidify their gains. The sheer numbers of Irish Americans gave them a power at the polls that few other immigrant groups in America had, and they used that power, combined with their loyalty and sense of

A family of Irish Americans gives expression to the hopelessness of their situation in this late nineteenth-century drawing.

community, to gain control of the largest cities in the country. Their strong sense of community helped them form labor unions that forced employers to ease some of the abusive conditions under which their parents had often been forced to work.

Once they had gained political power, there was little to stop Irish Americans from gaining access to the strata of society that had previously been denied to them. This ascent was hardly easy; in fact, the very characteristics that helped them gain political power and respect in the workplace—the intense clannishness and loyalty to one another—provoked negative reactions from those who already composed the upper crust of American society. Yet, by the late nineteenth century, the Irish were established in American society.

Contradictions

The story of Irish Americans' climb in American society is one of contradictions. On the one hand, they wanted to become part of the American establishment; on the other, they formed a closed, almost impenetrable community of their own. They worked in the homes of the wealthiest families in the country, yet few believed they deserved to have such elegant homes for themselves. Writer Peggy Noonan's aunt, Mary Jane, was an example of a servant who believed this. Noonan writes that her aunt worked as a lady's maid: "She loved what she would have called the fine things of the world but didn't aim for them, didn't seem to think they

were . . . her fate."[2] Irish Americans even mocked those individuals among themselves who tried to mimic the behavior of their betters, calling them "lace-curtain Irish."

Irish Americans also displayed contradictory behavior when fighting against discrimination and prejudice in their struggle for respectability, in turn practicing or advocating the same kind of discrimination against blacks and Chinese immigrants. For example, the Irish-owned and run newspaper the *Boston Pilot* promoted the idea that blacks were inferior and suited only to serving whites.

Respectability

Eventually the struggles of Irish Americans eased, and they gained the acceptance for which they had longed. Today, Americans of Irish descent hold some of the highest positions in government and business; they live in homes their desperate forebears, for all their scoffing at "lace-curtain Irish," could only dream of. So thoroughly have the descendants of Irish immigrants assimilated that few take time to acknowledge their heritage, except in the most perfunctory way. Whether this attitude would have greatly disturbed the Irish Famine immigrants is questionable. Most Irish Americans now live the very kind of life that immigrants such as William Porter from Ireland's County Down had in mind when he wrote home to his parents that "you have a chance of rising in the world here which you have not there and the fear of want is not always staring you in the face."[3]

CHAPTER ONE

Leaving Ireland

From the earliest days of colonial America, political oppression and poverty drove many Irish to seek their fortunes in the new land. Most of these early colonists were farmers or skilled laborers. Some came as indentured servants, willing to trade three to seven years of hard work in return for the cost of passage. Still, the prospect of wresting a living from the American wilderness discouraged all but relatively few Irish from risking what little they had.

By 1840 about 1 million people of Irish descent lived in the United States. By 1854, however, that number had more than doubled. The immigrants who arrived in this new wave were different from those who came before. A massive blight had devastated the staple crop in Ireland, the potato, resulting in famine. The immigrants who came during the mid-nineteenth century, therefore, were not just poor; they were desperate people who felt they had no choice but to leave the country they loved. Furthermore, unlike the Irish who had come earlier, 90 percent of the new arrivals were not Protestants but Catholics, who for generations had composed the dispossessed in Irish society. For these people, Ireland had long been a place of oppression and hopelessness; now it was a place where life itself had become virtually impossible.

The Irish Landowning System

Contributing to the desperation of Irish Catholics during the middle of the nineteenth century was a series of penal laws that had been imposed at the behest of the English by Ireland's parliament beginning in the late seventeenth century and which had systematically deprived them of their land. The laws declared that Catholics could no longer own land that was not already in their family, nor could they lease land. And although a landowner could, when he died, pass land he already owned to his sons, the land had to be divided equally among them. As a result, as time passed Catholics owned smaller and smaller parcels of land. And since a Catholic who wished to sell his land could sell only to Protestants, gradually more and more land went from Catholic to Protestant ownership.

One consequence of the penal laws was that by the early part of the nineteenth century Catholics owned only 7 percent of the land in Ireland, even though they made up more than 80 percent of the population. The penal laws were repealed in 1829, but by that time Catholics in Ireland were too poor to purchase their own land. Instead, they worked for English landowners, raising their crops and livestock and answering to agents the landowners had hired to oversee their estates. Irish peasants would work the land in return for a small wage and also rent small plots of land—maybe a half-acre or acre—for their own use, in the process giving most of their wages back to the landowners. On this land, tenant farmers grew what they needed to feed themselves

The Scotch Irish

More than a century before the Potato Famine, the Irish began to immigrate to what would one day be the United States. These colonists from Ireland were actually of Scottish heritage, having been encouraged by England's King James I to settle in Ireland during the 1600s. A combination of drought and economic hard times eventually motivated these "Scotch Irish" to pull up stakes again and seek a new start in England's American colonies. Many Scotch Irish went to what was then the frontier, settling in western Pennsylvania and the foothill regions of North Carolina and Virginia. During the nineteenth century they settled even farther west, crossing the mountains of Pennsylvania and traveling into Ohio, Kentucky, West Virginia, and Tennessee. The Scotch Irish, who were Protestant, had a relatively easy time assimilating into American communities. Long-simmering resentment between Protestants and Catholics in Ireland meant that when the largely Catholic famine immigrants began to arrive in America, the Scotch Irish were among those who were most hostile toward Irish Americans.

and their families. Those few tenant farmers who could afford to rent relatively large plots of perhaps a few acres would in turn rent smaller plots to poorer farmers. Under this system, some farmers barely grew enough on these tiny parcels of land to feed their families. This pattern of landownership entrapped millions of Irish, mostly Catholics, in grinding poverty.

Cottiers

Tenant farmers, or cottiers, as they were known, had few if any opportunities to earn cash for their labor. With what little remained of the menial wages they earned after they had paid their rent, some cottiers could afford to buy a piglet or a calf once a year. After raising the animal, they could sell it for the money they needed to buy necessities, such as cloth or a cooking pot. Occasionally they might have a surplus of crops to sell as well, but there was never money enough to pay for luxuries.

Indeed, cottiers had little in the way of creature comforts. Their cottages were simple dwellings, consisting of one room. The walls of the cottages were made of a combination of mud and stone, or sometimes just packed earth, and the roof was a series of crisscrossed tree limbs with the leaves still on them, although some cottages had more elaborately thatched roofs. Most cottiers owned little if any furniture. They slept on hay piled on the bare earthen floors, and many cottiers did not even have a covering to pull over them when they slept. A writer for the *Illustrated London News* visited one such cottage in 1843 and described it as "on the same scale of comfort as

the hut of the Esquimaux [Eskimo], or the wigwam of the North American Indian."[4]

Some peasants did not even have a cottage. These laborers, many of them single men, leased only an acre or so of land and lived in shacks, under bridges, or simply slept in ditches. Some men did not lease any land and instead traveled throughout the countryside finding what work they could. They were paid with a meal or two a day, and they slept in barns or out in the open.

Although cottiers did not own the land they lived on, their sons could inherit the right to lease that land. But just as was true of land owned by Catholics, the leased land

A family of cottiers poses outside their thatched-roof cottage. Cottiers earned very little and could afford no luxuries.

had to be divided equally among a cottier's sons. Very quickly the land available for an individual family could not produce adequate food to feed a family, so gradually people were forced to leave their land just to survive.

The Crops They Grew

For those cottiers who managed to remain on the land, there were few choices of what crop to grow. Farmers had tried planting several kinds of crops on their rented parcels over the years, but the one that grew best in Ireland's rocky soil and

damp climate was the potato. Potatoes were filling and nutritious, and millions of Irish depended on them for survival. They baked them, roasted them over fires, and added them to soups and stews.

In the cottier's household, meat was more of a flavoring than an ingredient. The *Illustrated London News* writer reported how a family he visited made use of a small piece of bacon: "The most they do is hang it in their chimney, and let it drip on their potatoes, each poor creature in turn pointing a potato to receive the dropping grease. This meal is called *'potatoes and point.'"*[5] The 900,000 or more families of cottiers ate potatoes almost exclusively, and 3 million people depended on potatoes but added a few other items, such as fish, to their diets. Most Irish farmers ate about six to nine pounds of potatoes per person each day.

The land that the Irish spent most of their time farming, though, belonged to the English landlords, who looked to that land as a source of income. Some potatoes were grown on that land, but much of it was used to grow grain and raise livestock, and most of these crops were sold and exported to England. Gradually, landlords began to search for ways to increase the acreage available for these moneymaking crops. By removing tenants, cereal crops and livestock could be raised on the vacated land.

The Poor Law of 1838

British tax laws provided even more incentive for landlords to force their tenants off the land. Landlords were taxed not only on the value of their Irish estates but also on the number of people who lived on the estate and leased land worth less than four pounds. Because so many cottiers leased parcels that were certainly worth less than four pounds, landlords saw evicting tenants as a simple way of both increasing income and reducing expenses.

As the number of families made homeless by evictions multiplied, Parliament in 1838 passed the Poor Law, which established workhouses where, in return for a place to sleep and food to eat, people did various jobs. Men were assigned chores that included breaking rocks or crushing animal bones to make fertilizer, and women often spent their days knitting. But as difficult as the evictions were for tenant farmers, far more devastating was a natural phenomenon that first occurred in 1845. That year, a fungus infected the potato crop, and even those who still had homes saw their food supply vanish almost overnight.

The Potato Blight

The disease that would eventually virtually eradicate Ireland's food supply had been seen before. In 1844 a potato blight had hit England and some parts of Europe. That year, Ireland's potato crop had seemed

This modern-day Irish farmer harvests potatoes in much the same way as his cottier forebears did.

unaffected by the disease, but by autumn 1845 it became clear that Ireland was in for trouble. An article in the October 18, 1845, edition of the *Illustrated London News* said that the disease was "extending far and wide" and went on to report that John Chester, in a letter to the *Dublin Evening Post,* "states that he has a field of twenty acres of potatoes, which, up to the 3rd instant, had been perfectly dry and sound, when they were attacked by the blight, and three-fourths of them are so diseased and rotten that pigs decline to eat them."[6]

Alarm quickly spread. The *Belfast News Letter* reported, "It may be here stated, once for all, that there is hardly a district in Ireland in which the potato crops at present are uninfected—perhaps we might say, *hardly a field.*"[7] That report was something of an overstatement, and in fact, only about 30 to 40 percent of the potato crop was ruined in 1845; but in 1846 the crop was devastated. Nearly all potatoes in Ireland were ruined.

The culprit was a fungus named *Phytopthora infestans,* which found damp climates such as Ireland's ideal. First the leaves of affected plants would turn black, then the stems would follow suit. The potatoes would look normal when harvested, but in storage the fungus continued its attack, turning the starch in the potato into sugar. The potatoes would rot, and the end result was a pulpy mass with a horrible smell.

The spores of the fungus were carried through the air, so the disease spread rapidly. Some people tried to save their crops by covering potato fields with cloth, hoping to keep the fungus away. Others cut affected potatoes into pieces and soaked them in water or tried drying the potatoes in an oven or leaving them out in the sun. None of these tactics stopped the fungus from working its destruction.

Some people tried to eat the affected potatoes, but by the time the diseased parts had been removed, there was little left. In 1845 an English observer wrote of Irish children's efforts to prepare the blighted potatoes: "They first peel off the skin, then they scoop out the black or diseased spots on all sides, as the disease enters the potato at different depths. It has rather a curious appearance when cleared of all the black spots, and even it looks much worse boiled than raw."[8]

The Great Hunger

By the autumn of 1846, Ireland was in the grip of famine. People called it *an gorta mór* (Gaelic for "the great hunger"). No one in Ireland was immune to the effects of the famine. In its September 4, 1846, edition, the *Cork Examiner* proclaimed, "All is alarm and apprehension. The landlord trembles for the consequences; so does the middleman; so does the tenant farmer."[9]

Throughout the countryside, civil disturbance erupted as people began to panic. They rioted when government officials appeared in an attempt to assess the situation and when tax collectors arrived. In the town of Youghal, located on the southeastern coast, a group of laborers tried to stop a shipment of corn that was leaving the harbor, angry that food was being exported while the people of Ireland starved. Later the same day, the mob destroyed shops that milled flour and made bread. In the town of Cloyne on September 25, the *Cork Examiner* reported that a mob of angry laborers after exhibiting their force for the purpose of intimidating the shopkeepers, proceeded to rifle the flour and provision shops. The bakers, seeing that resistance was completely useless, thought they might as well permit it with a good grace, and for the purpose of protecting their remaining property, generously distributed their loaves to the hungry claimants who retired without committing any further injury.[10]

Others ate whatever they could. Some ate grass, although in reality it provided no nutrition to humans. Those who lived near the seashore collected seaweed and made a meal of that. Called *dhoolamaun,* the dish consisted of boiled seaweed mixed with what little cornmeal or flour the people could obtain. One starving man was found chewing on a chunk of sod. One family seriously considered killing and cooking their cat, but they were unsure the cat meat would be safe to eat. Some were able to find cabbage to eat, but eating only cabbage gave them severe diarrhea, and the resulting dehydration could be deadly.

Members of an Irish farm family left destitute by the potato blight ponder their predicament.

During the Potato Famine, Irish peasants were forced to find nourishment wherever they could. Here, farmers gather seaweed to prepare the dish known as dhoolamaun.

Tumbling and Eviction

Meanwhile, some landlords saw the famine as an opportunity to finally evict their tenants, who, weak from hunger, were unable to work and pay their rent. The landlords also raised the rents of the farmers who were subleasing to other farmers. To pay the higher rent, these farmers would evict cottiers who were their tenants and plant cash crops such as wheat and corn on the vacated land. In this way, the famine imposed the greatest hardship on the poorest people.

When evicting tenants from their homes, landlords often hired men or called in soldiers to systematically remove them. The process was called "tumbling" or "shoveling out." Tenants would be given a short time—sometimes only minutes—to gather

their meager belongings. Then the men climbed up and "tumbled" down the thatched roofs, sometimes even the walls, to force tenants to leave. One woman, Bridget O'Donnel, was evicted in 1849. She described it this way: "Dan Sheedey and five or six men came to tumble my house; they wanted me to give possession. I said that I would not. . . . They commenced knocking down the house, and had half of it knocked down when two neighbours, women, Nell Spellesley and Kate How, carried me out."[11]

When a reporter for the *Illustrated London News* toured Ireland in 1849, after most of the evictions had already occurred, he commented on the many tumbled homes he encountered and on the effect the practice had on tenants:

To Tullig from Kilkee, I counted ninety-two roofless houses. Passing afterwards through the picturesque village of Cariegaholt to Donagha and Querin, I counted 105 dwellings in ruins. Clarefield, to which I came next, baffles description. Adults, who appeared idiotic; children, wrinkled with care, so that they appeared like aged persons; and men who should not be worn out, but more helpless than children, with scarcely a rag to cover them, crowded the place. Their habitations were mere kennels.[12]

Living in Desperation

The landlords were not obliged to provide any alternative shelter for the evicted tenants, who were forced to construct makeshift homes for themselves. One kind of home was called a *scalpeen* and was made from the remains of tumbled cottages. *Scalpeen* dwellers sometimes went around to other abandoned cottages and took what they could from them—a cooking pot here, a chair there. Another kind of dwelling, a *scalp,* was a hole dug in the earth, only a few feet deep, with a crude root made of turf. One observer described a *scalp* as resembling an inverted saucer. This same reporter noted that as bad as conditions for cottiers had been in the past, they were now much worse:

The mud cabins and turf huts that the peasantry lived in before 1846 were denounced by every traveler as the scandal of civilized Europe; and it was supposed that worse habitations

Evicted for not paying their rent, a family of tenants sits among their belongings. A constable waits at the entrance to the house to prevent reentry.

were not in the earth; but the Irish have proved that in their lowest deep there is still a lower deep—that a Scalpeen is worse than a mud-hut, and Scalp worse than a Scalpeen.[13]

In the city of Cork, entire families lived near the wharf in hogsheads—large barrels used to transport goods. The *Cork Examiner* reported on March 19, 1847, that some people "find it their soul refuge, not quitting it even during the night, except, perhaps, to straighten their limbs. In several hogsheads, four or five children, with their mother, are thus lodged, wedged and packed together, the young tenants half suffocated and struggling and fighting in their prison."[14]

Some landlords provided a little relief by allowing their tenants to remain on the land. In November 1846, for example, it was reported that Lady Carbery, "in consideration of the loss her tenants have sustained this year, intends to make no demand for rent on her extensive estates in this county."[15] But with so many desperate people roaming the land, some landlords feared for their lives, and with good reason: A few were shot and killed by angry tenants or former tenants.

The Poor Law Extension Act

Even as conditions in Ireland were reaching crisis proportions, the English were losing sympathy for the famine victims. Most of the English were Protestants and had a dim view of Catholics in general and Irish Catholics in particular. Many, in fact, saw the famine as a sign of God's displeasure with Ireland's Catholics. Moreover, many English viewed the nation's misery as just punishment for what they considered the Irish people's lazy and shiftless ways.

Official English policies treated the famine as Ireland's problem, even though England considered itself and Ireland a single country. The Poor Law Extension Act, passed in 1847, provided for the establishment of more workhouses in Ireland to give

A "Horrid Spectacle"

The September 15, 1847, edition of the newspaper the *Cork Examiner* contained an article about the destitution of people evicted from their homes. One section of the article describes how families in the Irish town of Dungarvan, who were driven to taking refuge in ditches, lived:

> Their mode of living levels them almost with brutes. At one quarter, where a bank of stones runs along a high-road, they have formed in it cells of a few feet wide. . . . Pent up in such dens, fever preys incessantly upon the bodies of such miserable creatures. It appears that the magistrates . . . tried to repress them by the powers of the new vagrancy law; but from the numbers to be dealt with, after the first display of legal severity, that attempt had to be abandoned, as absurd and inhuman.

the homeless a place to go, but the workhouses were now paid for by a tax paid by landowners. The Act made conditions worse for the remaining cottiers since it also contained a clause stating that anyone who held the rights to a quarter acre or more of land could not enter a workhouse.

The quarter-acre exclusion put many cottiers in a predicament. If they did not go to the workhouse, their families would starve. But in order to go to the workhouse, they had to turn over their land to the landlord. With no real choice, many abandoned their homes and went to the workhouse, where at least they knew they would be fed.

Workhouses soon became overcrowded, and conditions were so bad that the Irish called the road to the workhouse *Cosan no Marbh*—the "Pathway to the Dead." Disease was a constant presence in the workhouses, and about 25 percent of those who went to live in one died there from cholera, dysentery, or typhus. In 1847 a report on workhouse conditions stated,

> The building we found most dilapidated, and fast advancing to ruin, everything out of repair, the yards undrained and filled, in common with the cesspools, by accumulation of filth—a violation of all sanitary requirements; fever and dysentery prevailing throughout the house, every ward filthy to a most noisome degree . . . the paupers defectively

A landlord distributes clothing to victims of the Famine. Such instances of kindness were extremely rare, as most landlords cared little for the plight of their tenants.

Starving peasants clamor to be admitted to a workhouse. Overcrowding caused disease to run rampant in such places.

clothed, and many of those recently admitted continuing in their own rags and impurity.[16]

Despite the appalling conditions, by 1851 more than three hundred thousand people lived in workhouses, and more were waiting to get in.

Relief Efforts

Besides opening workhouses, the English government made sporadic attempts to feed people in soup kitchens around the country. Quakers living in Ireland also opened many soup kitchens, and by July 1847 about two thousand soup kitchens existed, serving hot meals to about 3 million people a day. The fare at such places was anything but lavish. Some kitchens actually served soup, but most served a dish called "stirabout," which was porridge made from oatmeal or corn.

Small amounts of monetary aid also came from other countries. In 1847 voluntary contributions worth $50,000 from the United States, particularly from New York and New Jersey, were collected and sent to Ireland. The Choctaw tribe of Native

Americans sent $710. People in Calcutta, India, contributed 16,500 pounds sterling; collections from another Indian city, Bombay, totaled 3,000 pounds sterling. Other countries also contributed to famine relief, including Italy, France, and Jamaica. Besides money, volunteers gathered and shipped clothing and food to Ireland.

Continued Misery

In spite of the help, the misery grew in Ireland. The blight was less severe in 1847, but because nearly the entire crop had been ruined in 1846, there were few seed potatoes to plant. As a result, the 1847 crop was meager. Then, in 1848, the blight came back and was nearly as bad as it had been in 1846. The famine continued until 1850, when the blight disappeared as suddenly as it had appeared.

As a direct result of the famine, nearly a million people died of starvation and sickness in Ireland between the years 1846 and 1851. At first the newspapers

Saying Goodbye

A writer for the *Illustrated London News* wrote in that publication's May 10, 1851, edition about his experience roaming the Irish countryside with a priest who was saying goodbye to an entire village of parishioners who were emigrating.

In company with one of these humble but exemplary men, I came to a sharp turn in the road, in view of that for which we sought . . . namely, the packing and making ready of, I may say, an entire village—for there were not more than half-a-dozen houses on the spot, and all their former inmates were preparing to leave. Immediately that my rev. friend was recognised, the people gathered about him in the most affectionate manner. He had a word of advice to Pat, a caution to Nelly, a suggestion to Mick; and he made a promise to Dan to take care of the "old woman," until the five pounds came in the spring to his 'Reverence' to send her over to America. Then ensued a scene of tears and lamentation, such as might have softened a much harder heart than mine or that of the priest. He stood for awhile surrounded by the old and the young, the strong and the infirm, on bended knees, and he turned his moistened eyes towards heaven, and asked the blessing of the Almighty upon the wanderers during their long and weary journey. Many were the tears brushed quietly away from the sunburnt cheeks of those who there knelt, and had implicit faith that the benediction so fervently and piously asked, would be vouchsafed to them.

dutifully reported each case of starvation. On October 30, 1846, for example, the *Cork Examiner* reported the death of one victim, Daniel Hayes, "who for several days subsisted almost on the refuse of vegetables, and went out on Friday morning in quest of something in the shape of food, but he had not gone far when he was obliged to lie down, and, melancholy to relate, was found dead some time afterward."[17] Eventually, though, the number of deaths became so high that newspapers went from reporting each shocking death to bemoaning the fact that the dead were so numerous that there were not enough coffins to go around.

The shortage of coffins resulted in a practice that appalled many observers. It was reported that in the parish of Kilmoe, a coffin was being used over and over. A corpse would be placed inside the coffin and taken to the cemetery, where the bottom of the coffin would open and the corpse would drop into the grave. The coffin was taken to pick up the next body, and the process was repeated.

Emigration

In the end, the Great Hunger left many Irish with only one choice: stay and starve, or leave and live. Many decided to leave, and during the famine years, at least 1 million people emigrated from Ireland to the United States. Few knew what they would do there, but they knew that at least they could find work and food. Many would probably have agreed with one American who went to Ireland and upon his return reported to the U.S. Senate what he had seen there: "There is nothing unnatural in the desire of the unfortunate Irish to abandon their cheerless and damp cottages, and to crawl inch by inch, while they have yet a little strength, from the graves which apparently yawn for their bodies."[18] And so began the great migration of Irish to the United States.

CHAPTER TWO

Sailing to America

Most of those who fled Ireland during the famine were stepping into the unknown. The majority had never set foot outside their county—some had never even been outside their village. Leaving their homeland was a decision made out of desperation, and making that decision was just the first step in a long process. Getting to America was a long and difficult journey, one often filled with peril.

Financing the Journey

Once they had decided to leave Ireland, emigrants had to come up with a way to finance their journey. Some pawned whatever they had—bedding, cooking pots, utensils—and used the money to buy tickets. Some sold all of their clothing, except what they were wearing, or sold their pig or cow, if they still owned one. Then they went to the local priest to be blessed.

The night before the emigrants were to leave, their friends held for them what was called "an America wake"—what amounted to a funeral wake for those going to America. Such a celebration was appropriate since their departure was like a death, in that many would never see their loved ones again.

The emigrants then piled their meager belongings into handcarts or stuffed them into bags and headed for a seaport.

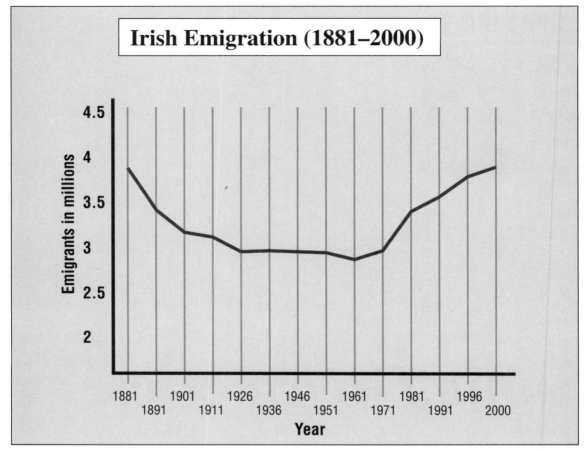

Irish Emigration (1881–2000)

Approximately three-quarters of the emigrants went to Dublin, where they boarded ships and sailed across the Irish Sea to Liverpool, England, where they then found passage on a ship to America. The remaining one-quarter sailed from the Irish ports of Galway, Limerick, or Cork.

Often, family members accompanied emigrants to the docks and watched as they boarded ships and sailed away. They stood on shore weeping and wailing as their sons and daughters left for a foreign land.

Those sailing to Liverpool took whatever transportation across the sea they could find. Many crossed on steamers, but emigrants also sailed away on fishing boats and barges, sometimes sharing space with food and livestock being exported to England. The voyage, which took twenty-two to thirty-six hours, was often miserable. In most cases, passengers were forced to remain on the top deck, rain or shine, night or day. During heavy rainstorms, the crew would sometimes throw a large tarp over the passengers, but they were otherwise exposed to the elements. On a steamer, as many as seven hundred people sometimes huddled on the deck. Most of them had never before been on a ship, and many became seasick.

Liverpool

Because the crossing was so difficult, emigrants were relieved to disembark on the docks of Liverpool. But their joy at leaving the ship was often short-lived; now they had to face even more peril, usually of the human variety. Those who met the bedraggled emigrants often were looking for easy marks, or people they could swindle. Few emigrants, especially during the first year of the famine emigration, were prepared to deal with the con men who awaited them.

The first group of tricksters that emigrants would encounter were called runners. These men would race to the docks as soon as they spotted a ship arriving from Ireland. As passengers left the ship, sometimes struggling to carry their bags, runners would approach them and, with a friendly smile, volunteer to help. Many emigrants gladly handed over their bags, grateful for assistance. But true to their name, some runners took off running, carrying with them everything the emigrants owned. Frederick Sabel, who ran a boardinghouse in Liverpool during the famine years, described the runners this way:

> The runners watch the steamboats night and day. Suppose a ship arrives at one o'clock in the morning, and it rains as fast as it can; the passengers are all

Irish emigrants disembark on the docks of Liverpool, the city from which most ships bound for America sailed.

frightened; everything is strange to them; and the moment the ship arrives, however many passengers there may be, there come as many runners, who snatch up their luggage as quickly as possible and carry it away; they are like so many pirates. If any of the passengers wish to keep on board the ship, they cannot; the police come and drive them away. . . . The people are actually driven with sticks into the hands of those people. . . . It is really a horrible thing.[19]

Some runners did not steal bags. Instead, they led the emigrants to a boardinghouse that they promised had excellent accommodations at good prices. These runners would quickly grab the emigrant's bags and walk away from the docks, leaving the emigrant with no choice but to follow. The runners often worked in concert with dishonest boardinghouse keepers and would direct the emigrants through the strange city into a building where rooms were rented. Once the emigrants were settled, the landlord would appear and demand a large amount of money for rent. The travelers, bewildered, would hand over the money.

Most emigrants planned to stay in Liverpool for a few days and had saved up what they thought would be enough money for rent. Some, though, were conned into handing over all of their money to the landlord. These unfortunate victims were forced to find low-paying jobs or even beg on the streets to make enough money to buy tickets for the voyage across the Atlantic—about ten dollars at the time. Caught up in the never-ending need to pay an unscrupulous landlord, some even

ended up staying in England permanently, living in poverty in Liverpool or eventually migrating to some other English city.

Conditions at the boardinghouses in Liverpool were often squalid at best. Many emigrants were forced to share a small room with as many as twenty other strangers. Some rooms were in basements, where almost no light penetrated. Some of the basements were filled with a foot or two of water all the time.

The migrants endured the foul living conditions, looking forward to the day when their ship would finally sail. However, many ships did not sail as scheduled. Although ticket agents promised that a ship would sail on a certain date, the fact was that many sailed days, even weeks, later than advertised, as ship owners and their agents tried to fill the ship with as many passengers as possible.

As emigrants waited out the days in overcrowded boardinghouses, they would be forced to make their meager stores of food last for days longer than anticipated, eating only one small meal a day. Some, unsure of what would be provided aboard ship, had purchased food to take with them on the voyage but had to eat it while they waited. When the desperation and hunger that forced the emigrants to leave Ireland in the first place followed them to Liverpool, some emigrants slipped into depression or other forms of mental illness. A few became so distraught that they committed suicide.

Ticket brokers engaged in deceptions beyond concealing the fact that ships would often not sail as advertised. The brokers wanted to sell as many tickets as they could

Emigrants are packed tightly on the deck of a ship bound for the United States. Ticket brokers were notorious for overbooking ships.

because they received a commission on every ticket they sold, so they routinely sold tickets to far more people than the ship could hold. Fortunately, when it came time to board the ship, most captains paid little attention to the number of passengers, so often all of the passengers made the voyage, in spite of the overbooking.

Brokers sometimes even sold worthless tickets they printed themselves, keeping the entire fare. The migrants who presented these tickets at the dock were denied pas-sage and were then stuck in Liverpool, usually penniless. Other than the worthless ticket, they had no receipt or contract from the broker and had no choice but to remain in England while they tried to earn money to buy a legitimate ticket.

Boarding the Ship

In an effort to prevent epidemics at sea, those emigrants who had valid tickets were given a cursory medical inspection before they could board the ship. A handful of doctors hired to do the job sometimes saw as many as one thousand passengers a day. Thorough examinations were impossible to do for so many people, so the doctors would simply ask the passengers to stick out their tongues as they filed by. Only the very obviously sick were refused passage. One passenger, named Robert Whyte, made the voyage in 1847 and wrote in his diary about his experiences. He described the appearance of the immigrants on board the ship this way:

A more motley crowd I never beheld; of all ages, from the infant to the feeble grandsire and withered crone. . . .

Many of them appeared to me to be quite unfit to undergo the hardship of a long voyage, but they were inspected and passed by a doctor, although the captain protested against taking some of them. One old man was so infirm that he seemed to me to be in the last stage of consumption [tuberculosis].[20]

Boarding the ship could also be a dangerous undertaking. The process was far from orderly and organized; passengers were expected to board as quickly as possible, and panic often ensued when individuals were separated from families or when people became fearful that the ship would

Passengers in Liverpool anxiously await the opportunity to embark. The boarding process was typically chaotic and often dangerous.

fill before they were aboard. The narrow entrance to the gangway would be mobbed, so some passengers would try to scale the sides of the ship as friends or family members already on board reached over the rail to help them. Dr. J.J. Lancaster, one of the medical inspectors at Liverpool, observed, "Sometimes the passengers have to watch their opportunity, and when the ship gets near the entrance to the dock you may see men, women, and children clambering up the sides of the ship."[21] Sometimes the people climbing the sides of the ship fell into the water and drowned. Wealthy philanthropist Vere Foster wrote of the embarkation process,

There is no regularity or decency observed with regard to taking the passengers on board the ship; men and women were pulled in any side or end foremost, like so many bundles. I was getting myself in as quickly and as dexterously as I could when I was laid hold of by the legs and pulled, head foremost down upon the deck, and the next man was pulled down on top of me. I was some minutes before I recovered my hat which was crushed flat as a pancake. The porters in their treatment of passengers, naturally, look only to getting as much money as they possibly can from them in the shortest space of time, and heap upon them all kinds of filthy and blasphemous abuse, there being no police regulations and the officers of the ship taking the lead in the ill-treatment of the passengers.[22]

Irish women and their daughters pass the time on a wooden bunk belowdecks.

Conditions on Board

Even though they transported thousands of immigrants, many of the ships used during the peak of famine emigration were not actually meant to carry passengers. They were instead designed to bring cargo such as timber, cotton, and tobacco from the United States to England, and then they were quickly fitted to carry immigrants on the return voyage.

Nearly all Irish emigrants traveled in steerage, which was the least expensive accomodation. Steerage passengers were

Dancing with Delight

Although there were often misery and sickness aboard ships, the passengers bound for the United States entertained themselves as best they could. A writer for the July 6, 1850, edition of the *Illustrated London News* reported the following to his readers:

> The scenes that occur between decks on the day before the sailing of a packet, and during the time that a ship may be unavoidably detained in dock, are not generally of a character to impress the spectator with the idea of any great or overwhelming grief on the part of the emigrants at leaving the old country. On the contrary, all is bustle, excitement, and merriment. The scene of a party of emigrants, male and female, dancing between decks—to the music of a violin— played for their amusement, by some of their fellow passengers, is not a rare one. Sometimes a passenger is skilful upon the Irish bagpipe, and his services are freely asked and freely given for the gratification of his countrymen and countrywomen—not simply while in dock, but, according to the reports of captains and others, during the whole voyage. Any person who can play the violin—the flute—the pipe, or any other instrument, becomes of interest and importance to the passengers, and is kept in constant requisition for their amusement. . . . Gray headed men and women are frequently to be seen dancing with as much delight. . . as if Seventeen, not Seventy, was the number that would most nearly express their age.

quartered on a deck low in the ship's hull, where there was no light or fresh air. A steerage ticket entitled a passenger to one-quarter of a berth, and berths were usually six feet by six feet. The berths were made of wood and lined the sides of the ship like shelves. Single passengers slept next to strangers—unmarried men next to unmarried women, old people next to children. Some women refused to get into the bunks to sleep next to a strange man and would sit up night after night, trying to fall asleep astride a trunk or leaning against a box.

In 1847 an English philanthropist, Steven de Vere, sailed in steerage to get an idea of what most emigrants had to endure and wrote of his experience:

> Before the emigrant has passed a week at sea he is an altered man. How can it be otherwise? Hundreds of poor people, men, women, and children, of all ages, from the driveling idiot of ninety to the babe just born, huddled together

without light, without air, wallowing in filth and breathing a fetid atmosphere, sick in body, dispirited in heart.[23]

De Vere went on to describe how passengers who became ill were obliged to lie hour after hour on bunks so hard and narrow that they could not turn over to get into a different position. These unfortunates had no food unless another passenger brought some to them.

To make matters worse, hygiene on board ship was almost nonexistent. Water was scarce; what fresh water that was available was used for drinking and cooking, not for bathing. Toilet facilities were basic. On some ships there were outhouse-type toilets on deck that flushed into the sea, but some emigrants did not know how to use them because they had no such thing back in Ireland. When the weather was bad, passengers were not allowed up on deck, so they used chamberpots. Often, though, the heaving of the ship sloshed the contents of the pots onto the floor, and the scarcity of water meant the resulting mess was difficult, if not impossible, to clean up.

Seasickness created another hygiene problem. Most passengers had never before been on a ship, and they would become seasick almost as soon as the ship sailed. They would become sickest when seas were rough, which was also the time they would be confined below deck. Many passengers would lie in their berth, lean over the edge, and vomit on whatever and whoever was below them.

Emigrants not only suffered from discomfort and illness but also from being victimized by some of their fellow passengers.

During the 1840s another man, Dr. J. Custis from Dublin, sailed on six emigrant voyages to get an idea of what those aboard had to endure, and then he wrote a series of newspaper articles about his experiences. Custis was particularly bothered by the crimes that took place, writing, "The torments of hell might, in some degree, resemble the sufferings of the emigrants on board. . . . Take all the stews [whorehouses] in Liverpool, concentrate in a given space the acts and deeds done in all for one year, and they would scarcely equal in atrocity the amount of crime committed in one emigrant ship during any single voyage."[24]

Shipboard crime was not unusual. Because passengers were forced to live close together, quarrels often broke out, and they soon turned to fistfights. Likewise, sexual assaults were not uncommon. Passengers also had to guard their few belongings closely; if they did not, another passenger searching for food or for goods to trade for money once in America would steal whatever they could find. One Englishman wrote that on his voyage he observed that they "prowled about" at night, and that if "you turn your head to one side it [one's belongings] vanished to be found no more."[25]

Getting Food and Water

Emigrants were victimized not just by their fellow passengers but also had to endure indignities (and worse) meted out by the ship's crew. During the 1840s British law required that each passenger aboard ship receive seven pounds of food a week and six pints of water a day. The water ration was meager enough since it was to be used for drinking, cooking, and washing.

But once at sea, the captain and crew often ignored the regulations or followed them arbitrarily. Vere Foster traveled on an emigrant ship, the *Washington,* during the late 1840s. With regard to water distribution aboard ship, he wrote,

> I went on board the next day and witnessed the first occasion of giving out the daily allowance of water to the passengers. In doing so there was no regularity, the whole 900 and odd passengers were called forward at once to receive their water pumped out into their cans from barrels on deck. The serving out of the water was twice capriciously stopped by the mates of the ship who, during the whole time without any provocation, cursed and abused and cuffed and kicked the passengers and their tin cans. And having served out water to about 30 persons, in two separate times, said they would give no more water out till the next morning, and kept their word.[26]

Food was also not always distributed as specified by law. Sometimes the captain withheld food until the ship actually set sail. Passengers might board the ship on a Wednesday, when the voyage was supposed to begin, but the ship might sit at the dock or in the harbor for days while waiting for favorable winds or for a storm to pass. Foster wrote that the day after passengers boarded,

> provisions were not served out this day, notwithstanding the engagement contained in our contract tickets, and notwithstanding that all the passengers were now on board, the most of them since yesterday and had no means of communication with the shore. Many of them being very poor, had entirely relied upon the faithful observance of the promise contained in their tickets, the price of which includes payment for the weekly allowance of provisions.[27]

New York's Medical Inspection

No central authority dictated how healthy immigrants had to be in order to be allowed to disembark, but some port cities did at least provide for medical inspection of new arrivals. For example, New York had a quarantine law starting in about 1758 that required all ships to stop and anchor before allowing passengers to disembark. Once anchored, the ships were boarded by a doctor, who either pronounced the passengers healthy to leave or moved them to the marine hospital that had been built on Staten Island in 1799. Sometimes ships had to wait for days before the doctor would board, and while they waited, friends from shore were allowed to visit those on board, potentially spreading whatever disease that might infect the passengers.

The next day, Foster continued, food was still not distributed. Foster wrote a petition demanding that provisions be given out and asked many of the steerage passengers to sign it. When he tried to deliver the petition, however, the first mate punched him in the face and knocked him down.

When the weather permitted, immigrants were allowed up on deck, a few at a time, to build fires in crudely constructed stoves and cook their food. Passenger Robert Whyte described fireplaces as being inside large wooden crates lined with bricks. All day long, he continues, the fires were surrounded by people, some making a kind of stew in large pots and others baking cakes on griddles. The cakes, he goes on to say, were burnt on the outside but usually not cooked on the inside. Some people had herring or bacon to eat as well as cakes and hardtack biscuits.

Coffin Ships

Many who boarded ships were sick before they ever set foot on deck, victims of illnesses contracted in Ireland or in an overcrowded Liverpool boardinghouse. In the crowded, unsanitary conditions on board, disease spread quickly. One of the most common shipboard diseases was typhus, which was spread by the ticks and fleas that infested the holds of many ships. At least thirty thousand Irish emigrants died of the disease either during the voyage or soon after disembarking. Dysentery, which causes severe diarrhea, also killed many, particularly young children, for whom the attendant dehydration is particularly dangerous. For many passengers, disease finished the job begun by malnutrition. Because so many passengers died during voyages, ships that carried famine immigrants were called coffin ships.

Many Irish Catholic immigrants were buried at sea during those years, mostly without a proper funeral or last rites, since a priest was usually not available. For families, the lack of a proper religious ceremony made their loss twice as hard to bear. Foster wrote on November 25, 1850, that

another child, making about 12 in all, [had] died of dysentery or want of proper nourishing food and was thrown

A replica of an emigrant ship is moored at Blennerville, Ireland. Because so many passengers died during the ocean crossing, such vessels were called coffin ships.

"Health and Comfort All Among Them"

In 1850 a writer for the *Illustrated London News* wrote a series of articles about Irish emigration. In one article, he describes the embarkation of the passengers and lists the provisions that the British government requires ships to supply to the emigrants.

> Many of them bring, in addition to boxes and trunks containing their worldly wealth, considerable quantities of provisions, although it must be confessed that the scale fixed by the Government to be supplied to them by the ship is sufficiently liberal to keep in health and comfort all among them, who, in their ordinary course of life, were not accustomed to animal food. The following is the scale in addition to any provision which the passengers may themselves bring: 3 quarts of water daily; 2 and ½ pounds of bread or biscuit (not inferior to navy biscuit); 1 pound wheat flour; 5 pounds oatmeal; 2 pounds rice; 2 ounces tea; ½ pound sugar; ½ pound molasses.

These provisions were to be issued in advance, at least twice a week. The writer also states that "Vessels carrying as many as 100 passengers must be provided with a seafaring person to act as passenger's cook, and also with a proper cooking apparatus. A convenient place must be set apart on deck for cooking, and a proper supply of fuel shipped for the voyage." Rules such as these were not always enforced, though; once a ship set sail, the government had no way of knowing whether the ship captain was following the law, and once the passengers were taken to their destination, they were more concerned with the future, not with the past voyage.

into the sea sewn up, along with a great stone, in a cloth. No funeral service has yet been performed, the doctor informs me, over anyone who has died on board; the Catholics objecting, as he says, to the performance of any such service by a layman.[28]

With no priest available, Catholic emigrants were also unable to attend mass. However, informal religious services were held. Whyte observed one of these:

> In the evening they [the emigrants] had prayers in the hold and were divided

into two parties—those who spoke Irish, and those who did not; each section having a leader who gabbled in his respective language a number of 'Paters' and 'Aves', as quickly as the devotees could count their beads. After these religious exercises they came back upon deck and spent the remainder of the day jesting, laughing and singing.[29]

Even as they lamented the hardships the emigrants endured, some observers blamed them, claiming that they had brought misfortune on themselves. On May 19, 1847, for example, the *Cork Examiner,* knowing that people still in Ireland would be interested in the fate of the emigrants, printed an excerpt from the New York *Sun* that referred to the hardship people encountered aboard ship:

The paupers who have recently arrived from Europe give a most melancholy account of their sufferings. Upwards of eighty individuals, almost dead with the ship fever, were landed from one ship alone, while twenty-seven of the cargo died on the passage, and were thrown into the sea. They were one hundred days tossing to and fro upon the ocean, and for the last twenty days their only food consisted of a few ounces of meal per day, and their only water obtained from the clouds. The miseries which these people suffer are brought upon themselves, for they have no business to leave their country without at least

a sufficient quantity of food to feed them while making the passage.[30]

The Passenger Acts

In reaction to the conditions aboard the emigrant ships, both Great Britain and the United States attempted to reform the already-existing Passenger Acts. Earlier acts required captains to provide a specific amount of food per person—about one pound per day for each passenger. In 1849 the Passenger Acts were amended to include tea, sugar, and molasses, which had previously been considered luxuries, to be distributed twice a week. The amendments also called for larger bunks: Instead of the twenty-inch-wide bunks that were typical, ships now had to provide twenty-four-inch-wide bunks. As a result of the reforms, fares rose, but shipboard conditions improved. Although passengers crossing the Atlantic were still subject to seasickness and contagious diseases, they were much more likely to survive the voyage than they would have been in earlier years. Many had crossings similar to that of Samuel Laird, who wrote to his mother in May 1850 after arriving in Philadelphia: "I am safely arrived after a passage of 28 days, nothing transpired worth noticing on the passage only one great blessing that we all enjoyed good health."[31]

No matter what hardships they suffered during the voyage, these were only the first of many challenges the emigrants would face. Their next challenge was making themselves at home in their new country.

CHAPTER THREE

Making a Home

After embarking on a long and often perilous journey from Ireland to America, weary travelers were thrilled at the sight of their new homeland. Combined with their excitement at making a new life in a new land, however, were feelings of confusion and fear. Nearly everything Irish immigrants encountered in America was new and strange, and the only security lay in sticking together. For this reason, most Irish immigrants in the United States gravitated to cities that were home to Irish who had arrived earlier.

Confused and Frightened

The immigrants' first few hours in the United States left them feeling confused and frightened. There would be no formal processing center for immigrants until 1855, when the state of New York opened a center called Castle Garden, located at the southern tip of Manhattan and run by the New York State Commission of Emigration. The only requirement dating to 1824 was that a ship's captain report to New York City Officials the name, birthplace, last known residence, age, and occupation of each immigrant on his ship. Besides registering this information with the captain—and in other U.S. cities, this information was not even required—immigrants were also directed to pay what was called "hospital money" of $1.50. Payment of the fee was a kind of insurance, entitling them to treatment at a city-owned hospital for an entire year.

Other than those two brief procedures, immigrants who arrived in New York during the late 1840s and early 1850s simply stepped off the boat and onto the streets. If they were lucky and their ship's arrival time had been posted, they might be met by friends or relatives who had preceded them. Usually, though, they wandered off the ships, unsure of what to do or where to go next.

Runners and Con Men

Sometimes even before they paid the hospital fee, immigrants encountered runners similar to those the immigrants had encountered in Liverpool. These runners did not wait on the docks in New York; instead, they would jump on the boats that were used to ferry immigrants ashore and accost the new arrivals even before they had set foot on dry land.

Beginning in 1847, New York runners were required to purchase licenses to ply their trade and they wore badges indicating that they were "official." This did nothing to change their behavior toward immigrants, however. Still, because they wore official-looking badges, immigrants were more likely than before to trust them, and the runners continued to defraud as many people as they could find. One man, for example, immigrant William Lalor, wrote home about his troubles with runners and others who defrauded him, acknowledging that part of the problem was his "total ignorance of the ways, manners, customs, prices . . . of the country by which I got fooled out of all my money within three weeks after landing."[32]

Often, these runners were fellow Irishmen who used their Irish background to con newly arrived Irish immigrants into giving them their bags or following them to

Immigrants are shown arriving in New York in this 1847 painting. Swindlers bent on victimizing the new arrivals were plentiful.

overpriced accommodations. One account details the predicament a young man arriving in New York with a box of tools and a bundle of clothes found himself in:

> The moment he landed, his luggage was pounced upon by two runners, one seizing the box of tools, the other confiscating the clothes. The future American citizen assured his obliging friends that he was quite capable of carrying his own luggage; but no, they should relieve him . . . of that trouble. Each was in the interest of a different boarding-house, and each insisted that the young Irishman with the red head should go with him. . . . Not being able to oblige both gentleman, he could only oblige one; and as the tools were more valuable than the clothes, he followed in the path of the gentleman who had secured that portion of the "plunder."[33]

To be a successful runner, one had to be strong and aggressive, and the good ones were well paid. One *New York Tribune* article written during that period said that a runner "must be a man, or rather a brute, that fire would not burn, rope hang, nor water drown; with a fist like a sledgehammer, and muscle enough to overthrow a bull. With such qualifications, in proportion to his smartness, he would receive from $50 to $100 a week from his employer the broker."[34] In 1851 alone, 1,712 emigrant ships arrived in New York, so the opportunities for runners to make a living were vast.

Runners also promised to help immigrants arrange for travel to their final destination, whether to another city or to unclaimed lands in the nation's interior. Often, however, these tickets for travel by railroad or canal barge were worthless forgeries or were for a destination far short of where the immigrant wished to go.

Everywhere the new arrivals turned, someone was prepared to take advantage of them. Money changers also frequented the docks, waiting to victimize unsuspecting immigrants hoping to exchange their British pounds and shillings for American dollars. The money changers charged high rates for their services and cheated the unsuspecting immigrants, who were unfamiliar with exchange rates and could ill afford to lose even a penny.

"This Wealthy Christian City"

The immigrants' disorientation was made all the worse by the disorder and confusion around them. Those who managed to avoid being conned by runners still found themselves wandering through streets ankle-deep in garbage. Occasionally, herds of wild pigs or packs of wild dogs, drawn to the refuse, would run by.

As darkness fell, immigrants with nowhere to spend the night would feel increasingly apprehensive. Some ended up sleeping on the sidewalks, with their bags for pillows, but most found shelter in boardinghouses, damp cellars, crowded apartments, single rooms, or shacks hastily built on the city's outskirts. Most of the lodgings teemed with flies, bedbugs, and rats. Lodgers shared beds, sometimes in shifts. One New York resident at the time

This sketch offers an idealized depiction of an Irish squatter community near New York's Central Park. In reality, life in such settlements was a good deal more severe.

wrote that "crazy old buildings—crowded near tenements in filthy yards—dark, damp basements—leaky garrets—shops, outhouses, and stables converted into dwellings though scarcely fit to shelter brutes—are the habitations of our fellowbeings, in this wealthy Christian city."[35] In one ten-room New York building, fourteen immigrant families made their home.

By 1850 more than thirty thousand Irish immigrants were living in basements in New York. Often these cellars flooded with sewage as the city's inadequate sewage system overflowed. As a result of the unsanitary conditions, diseases such as cholera and yellow fever spread quickly.

Few buildings had running water, so residents had to get water from fire hydrants on the streets or from one of New York's rivers. There was not enough water for bathing or washing clothes, and a few businesses opened specifically for that purpose, such as the People's Washing and Bathing Establishment in New York City. These businesses soon failed, though, probably because poor immigrants had money only for essentials such as shelter and food. Many of them bathed in the Hudson, Harlem, or East Rivers.

Toilet facilities were also inadequate and usually consisted of one outhouse, or privy, in a building's yard, which was to be used by all tenants. Because one privy could not withstand use by an entire building, the facilities overflowed into the yard. In New York, it was common to encounter waste water and sewage in alleys, yards, streets, and gutters.

Conditions were not much different for Irish immigrants who settled in other cities. From Boston to Charleston, South Carolina, to New Orleans, immigrants found that they were forced by poverty to live in the least desirable parts of town. In New Orleans, for example, the newly arrived Irish could only afford to live in low-lying areas, where disease-carrying mosquitoes bred in pools of stagnant water. Everywhere, accommodations were substandard, consisting of single rooms occupied by as many as thirty people, or cellars or attics— some with ceilings so low that an adult could not stand up straight. There was no sanitation system and no garbage pickup,

so rubbish was thrown out of windows into streets and yards. Hungry immigrants sometimes roamed the streets, foraging through trash for something to eat.

Many Irish immigrants settled in and around Boston. Some of the poorest immigrants sailed from Liverpool to Canada because the fare was cheaper than passage to the United States. The immigrants would then walk or find other transportation to Boston or elsewhere in New England. In fact, about seventy-three thousand famine immigrants sailed first to Canada, then immediately crossed the border into the United States and on to Boston. Of the arrival of Irish immigrants in Boston, historian Oscar Handlin says that they "crammed the city, recasting its boundaries

Irish immigrants disembark at Grosse Isle, Canada. Because the fare was so much cheaper, many Irish opted to sail to Canada and then to cross into the United States.

and disfiguring its physical appearance; by their poverty they introduced new problems of disease, vice, and crime, with which neither they nor the community were ready to cope."[36]

City leaders were not prepared for such an influx of new residents and were dismayed by the resulting overcrowding. For example, in 1848 city leaders in Boston commissioned a study on the living conditions among the Irish in order to find a way to combat the disease and death that spread through their tenements. The subsequent *Report of the Committee of Internal Health, Boston, 1849* found in some places "grown men and women sleeping together in the same apartment, and sometimes wife and husband, brothers and sisters, in the same bed."[37]

In every eastern and southern city, Irish immigrants were forced into the poorest neighborhoods. Many times, they lived in settlements of hastily built wooden shanties or shacks spread out on the outskirts of cities. One such settlement was in what is now Central Park in New York City. In addition to people, cows, pigs, goats, and chickens lived in these neighborhoods, which came to be known as "Irishtowns," or shantytowns. Other names were even more descriptive of conditions under which people lived; for example, one Irish slum in New York was known as Hell's Kitchen. In 1862 it was estimated that about twenty thousand immigrants lived as "squatters," meaning they paid no rent or taxes, in these settlements. The immigrants who lived in these shantytowns did whatever work they could find, such as ragpicking or preparing streets for paving by removing rocks.

Striking It Rich

A few lucky Irish immigrants literally struck gold. During the 1849 gold rush, many Irish immigrants who had the money to travel made their way west to seek their fortunes, as William V. Shannon notes in his book *The American Irish:*

> At a time when hundreds of thousands of Irish were packed in the slums of Boston's North End and New York's East Side and were looked down upon as laborers and kitchen help, other Irish of identical background were amassing millions from the Comstock Lode and the Montana copper mines, running the governments of Nevada and California, and setting the social tone of San Francisco's Nob Hill.

In San Francisco, for example, Irish immigrant Peter Donahue thought the city needed a gas lighting system, so he erected streetlights in the city. He built a mansion in downtown San Francisco and left an estate of $4 million when he died. James Phelan first worked as a grocery clerk in New York City but headed west during the gold rush. Eventually, he opened a saloon, then started a real estate business. He became one of the wealthiest men in San Francisco.

The Toll

Living in such poor conditions took a physical toll on the Irish immigrants. As a consequence, the average famine immigrant lived only about five or six years after arriving in the United States, often dying from diseases such as tuberculosis, typhoid, cholera, and pneumonia. The children of the immigrants were particularly hard-hit and suffered from many illnesses to which malnutrition and neglect contributed greatly. In New York 75 percent of deaths in 1857 were children under five years old.

The psychological stress that such living conditions imposed was high, resulting in various social problems such as alcohol abuse, prostitution, and mental illness. In New York City in 1859, for example, 55 percent of those arrested were Irish. Many of the arrests among the Irish were for drunk and disorderly behavior. When Irishwomen were arrested, it was often for prostitution; in fact, during the mid-nineteenth century the majority of the prostitutes in northern cities were Irish. Mental illness was common among Irish immigrants, brought on by malnutrition, disease, and stress.

Often, both parents in a family would die, leaving behind young children. When children were orphaned, few Irish Americans could afford to take them in, so these youngsters would take to the streets, begging and taking shelter wherever they could. Often, well-meaning citizens would step in to help the children, putting them on what were called "orphan trains" and sending them into rural areas and small towns where couples and families supposedly wanted to adopt children. By 1870, for example, about ten thousand children a year were being taken out of New York City. This practice distressed the largely Catholic Irish, who did not like the fact that the children were often placed in Protestant homes and were raised as Protestants. Moreover, rather than being made a part of a family, many of these children were put to work as farmhands or domestic servants.

The Urbanized Irish

Even though conditions in the cities were appalling, famine immigrants showed little interest in settling in rural areas. The vast majority of them had lived in rural Ireland, but in the United States, about three-quarters of Irish immigrants settled in urban areas. Some, especially those who came to the United States during the peak famine years, had no choice: When they arrived at port cities such Boston or New York, they could not afford to travel any farther. Even some who could have moved on did not, regarding cities as a refuge; they found comfort in being among large numbers of Irish people, whose customs and religion were familiar.

Another reason that many Irish did not settle in rural areas was that there were few Catholic churches in the rural areas of the United States. For Irish Catholics, the church had long been a center around which to build a life, and they wanted one nearby. And because discrimination and prejudice against Catholics was common in much of America, many Irish felt that it was better to live among other Irish, where one's religion was the norm and they knew they would be accepted.

Irish immigrants like these established sizable communities in a number of cities across the United States.

Perhaps, too, the very familiarity with farm life drove some Irish to stay in the cities. Some historians suggest that the Irish were not drawn to farming in the United States because it reminded them of the oppressive conditions that were forced upon them by their landlords on farms back in Ireland. Those memories, combined with unfamiliarity with American climate, soil, and farming technology, contributed to keeping the majority of Irish immigrants close by the cities where they landed.

By 1870 more Irish lived in New York City than anywhere else in America. Many had settled in the slums of lower Manhattan, such as the Five Points area, which was notorious for its crime and street gangs. Other cities that had large Irish communities were Philadelphia, Boston, Chicago, San Francisco, St. Louis, Jersey City, Pittsburgh, Providence, and Cleveland. Regardless of where they settled, the Irish displayed a remarkable ability to adapt to city living.

The Rural Settlers

Some of those who came to the United States from Ireland did settle in rural areas to farm. For example, Irish immigrants established farming communities in New York's Niagara River Valley during the 1860s and in Susquehanna County, Pennsylvania. Much of the midsection of the continent was considered the frontier during the mid-nineteenth century, but some of the more adventurous Irish did settle there. In the small towns and villages of the Midwest, Irish settled, taking jobs as blacksmiths, carpenters, clerks, tailors, gardeners, masons, and laborers.

The Catholic Church

Although the neighborhood provided a strong sense of security for Irish Americans, the most important institution in these communities was the Catholic Church. As a consequence, the Catholic Church grew tremendously in America. Before the famine immigrants arrived, the Catholic Church had only 663,000 members in America; by 1860, there were 3,103,000 Catholics in the United States.

Irish Catholics had left behind their small, rural villages for American cities, but they re-created a kind of small village in city neighborhoods, centered on the church. The Catholic Church helped the Irish maintain memories of home and a sense of identity. With this comfortable, familiar foundation, Irish immigrants felt better equipped to build new lives in America. And the church served not only as a religious center but also as the center of all aspects of life for many Irish. Andrew M. Greeley, a Catholic priest and writer living in the United States, says that the parish was

An Irish family lives on the street in New York's Five Points area, a district notorious for its gangs and high crime rate.

a symbol of loyalty around which the immigrants and their children and grandchildren could rally in a society that was at first hostile and then not especially friendly. For many of us, it is no exaggeration to say that the parish was the center of our lives; it provided us with education, recreation, entertainment, friendships, and potential spouses. It was a place to belong. When asked where we came from, we named the parish rather than the street or neighborhood.[38]

Lawrence J. McCaffrey, a professor at Loyola University and a leading authority on the Irish in America, notes that the church provided spiritual guidance and solace for the Irish: "Irish neighborhoods, focused around the Catholic parish, served as psychological havens, preserving faith, tradition, and values, perpetuating a sense of community that could have disintegrated into an oppressive situation."[39]

As the number of Catholic Irish in America rose, the matter of providing their children with a Catholic education became a concern. Early immigrants from Ireland felt that American schools were too Protestant: It was common, for example, for teachers to teach from the King James Bible, a version that was not approved by the Catholic Church's leaders in Rome. In response to this perceived shortcoming in American schools, the Irish community pooled its resources to pay to bring nuns from Ireland to teach in schools established in cities such as New York and Charleston, South Carolina.

A network of Catholic schools was only one of the Catholic-based institutions set up by the Irish in America. They soon established other social institutions to provide assistance for Irish Catholic immigrants. These included Catholic hospitals, also staffed by nuns from Ireland, and Catholic orphanages, which were created as an alternative to shipping children off to be raised by Protestants in far-off towns. This effort was particularly successful; by 1885 Catholic nuns were taking care of 80 percent of the orphaned children in New York City.

Helping Themselves

The Catholic Church was of vital importance in helping immigrants gain a foothold in America, but secular organizations set up by the Irish themselves provided aid as well. Even before the famine years, Irish immigrants who had settled in the United States in earlier years made some effort to

Chain Migration

The money they earned allowed Irish Americans, particularly single Irishwomen who did not have their own families to support, to join in the process of "chain migration," sending a portion of their wages back to Ireland each week or month. The money helped feed their loved ones back home and paid for the passage of family members to come to America. Many historians believe that money sent back to Ireland from Irish immigrants in the United States actually helped boost the Irish economy and bring it back from the devastating effects of the famine. Between 1848 and 1861, Irish American workers sent more than $60 million back to Ireland. The number may be even higher because not all of the money sent back was known about.

help newcomers avoid the ordeals that they had had to face. For example, a group of volunteers formed the Irish Emigrant Society in 1839 to help immigrants as they tried to settle into life in New York City. Members of the society would meet with immigrants soon after they arrived and provide them with advice and information. The society opened the Emigrant Savings Bank in 1850, and through that institution Irish Americans were able to send money to Ireland to pay for the passage of family members who had stayed behind. The society

Editorial cartoons, such as this one depicting Irish children kicking a copy of the King James Bible, decried immigrants establishing separate Catholic schools.

made a profit by keeping 12.5 percent of the money sent to Ireland.

The society also warned prospective emigrants still in Ireland that life in the United States would not be as easy as they might imagine. In 1849 the society published a leaflet that stated,

We desire, preliminarily, to caution you against entertaining any fantastic idea, such as that magnificence, ease, and health, are universally enjoyed in this country. . . . It is natural for persons who have adventured to leave home and to seek their fortunes in a foreign and distant country, to give highly coloured accounts of a success, which in reality, has been but the obtaining of a laborious employment.[40]

Gradually, as famine conditions eased in Ireland, Irish American organizations grew to meet the needs of the growing numbers of Irish women who, seeing little future in their poverty-stricken homeland, were emigrating. The women had led sheltered lives in Ireland and therefore were easy marks for a wide variety of con artists in America. During the 1850s the Women's Protective Emigration Society was formed to help female emigrants from Ireland. The society's volunteers helped young women find jobs or paid their fare to travel on to other cities to find work. Another organization, the New York Magdalen Female Benevolent Society, even provided women a place to live. Women housed there, though, were forced to follow strict rules. They had to get up at 5 A.M. in the summer, and the matron, a sort of house mother, would even dictate the clothes each resident would wear each day.

Also helping new arrivals negotiate the often-bewildering environment of American cities were several newspapers. As early as 1810, the *Shamrock* newspaper was operating in New York City. In 1836 the *Boston Pilot* began circulation in that city, offering job listings, news about the lives of the Irish in the United States, and articles about what was happening back in Ireland. Other cities, including Philadelphia and Charleston, South Carolina, also had newspapers specifically meant for Irish immigrants.

St. Patrick's Day

In Ireland, March 17 was originally celebrated as a holy day to honor St. Patrick, Ireland's patron saint. Over time, though, the day evolved from a holy one to a secular one.

The first parades held on St. Patrick's Day in the United States took place as early as 1737 in Boston and 1762 in New York, but they were simple and had a religious theme. St. Patrick's Day parades as we know them today began when anti-Catholic demonstrators in New York City paraded through the streets with effigies of St. Patrick on March 17. The effigies were called "Paddies" and were usually dressed in rags, their mouths smeared with molasses. Often, a string of potatoes ringed their necks and a bottle of whiskey was shoved into their pockets. To show their solidarity and to counteract the opposition, Irish Catholics, particularly members of the Ancient Order of Hibernians (AOH), marched through New York City in 1854 in a St. Patrick's Day parade. Because they feared violence from the Know-Nothings, the AOH was escorted by several Irish militia companies. The New York parade grew to the grand festival it is today, and many other cities in the United States have similar parades, including Boston; New Orleans; Savannah, Georgia; Orlando and Hollywood, Florida; and Tucson, Arizona.

Other organizations formed to provide social activities, as well as security, for Irish immigrants. The Ancient Order of Hibernians, for example, was a club that provided a chance for Irish immigrants to socialize. In addition, it helped them keep abreast of what was going on back in Ireland and among Irish immigrants in America. The Hibernians also provided life insurance policies at affordable prices. The Society of St. Vincent de Paul was organized in 1846 to preserve family life among poor Catholic immigrants and to provide them relief in the form of food, money, and medicine, among other things. Irish literary organizations were formed during the 1840s that provided, along with organized discussions about literature, disability and life insurance. And organizations known as county societies were founded in most large American cities and helped Irish Americans find others who had come from the same part of Ireland as they did. These county societies would hold dances, concerts, and picnics.

By the 1850s Irish Catholics in the United States had set up what historian Oscar Handlin calls "a society within a society." The institutions they established," he goes on to write, "had no counterpart in the Old World, where the community was a unified whole, adequately satisfying all the social desires of its members."[41] The all-inclusive society they developed in America meant that the Irish were, therefore, largely self-reliant. They rarely had to venture outside their communities for spiritual, social, or economic support.

Although this separation from the rest of society was in part not voluntary—after all, the Irish were not made to feel welcome in most parts of the United States—it quickly became the preferred way of life for most of the immigrants. This separation would prove difficult to overcome, even after its value to the Irish had ended. Many Americans already viewed these Irish immigrants with suspicion; the self-imposed isolation practiced by Irish Catholics did little to relieve those suspicions. But if more than a tiny minority of Irish Americans were to have any hope of escaping a seemingly endless cycle of poverty, they would have to get jobs that would earn a living wage. To do that, the Irish would have to overcome misconceptions and outright bigotry on the part of their fellow Americans.

CHAPTER FOUR

Working

esides finding a place to live, one of the first things Irish immigrants had to do after arriving in America was find work. Some immigrants had assistance from benevolent organizations in the cities they settled in, such as New York's Irish Emigrant Society or the Mission of Our Lady of the Rosary for the Protection of Irish Immigrant Girls. Others had friends or relatives who had already been in America for a while and could help them find work. The majority of immigrants, however, had few prospects for earning a living. And because most of them had few marketable skills, they were forced to take menial, sometimes dangerous, jobs.

Digging Canals

By the time the large influx of immigrants arrived during the 1840s and 1850s, some Irish Americans—those who had come several decades earlier—were hard at work, building the nation's transportation system. The Industrial Revolution was under way, creating a need to move both raw materials and finished goods long distances. Moreover, the nation was expanding, and more and more people needed to travel. Canals, roads, and railroads were all needed, and these earlier immigrants had found plenty of demand for their labor in building them.

Such construction jobs required only physical strength and a willingness to work long hours—qualities that Irishmen accustomed to farmwork back home had in abundance. Although many of their British landlords back in Ireland had disparaged the Irish as lazy, Americans were finding this to be an unfair characterization. One newspaper editor wrote early in the nineteenth century that "America demands for her development an inexhaustible fund of physical energy, and Ireland supplies the most part of it. There are several sorts of power working at the fabric of this Republic—waterpower, steam-power, and Irish power. The last works hardest of all."[42]

Long before the famine immigrants arrived, Irish workers had built the Erie Canal, which connects the Hudson River with Lake Erie, and as the nineteenth century progressed, Irish workers continued to dig canals, including the Wabash and Erie Canals in Indiana, Pennsylvania's Chesapeake and Ohio Canals, Connecticut's Enfield Canal, the Miami Canal in Ohio, and the Blackstone Canal in Rhode Island, among others. So many workers were needed that companies advertised for workers in Irish newspapers and would send agents to the docks in New York City to hire men as they walked off ships from Ireland.

Canal builders worked long and hard, often twelve to fifteen hours a day. And the work was dangerous: More than once the muddy canal banks collapsed as they were being dug, burying workers alive. Those who were not killed or injured in construction accidents were often laid low by diseases such as cholera or malaria, which they contracted while working and living

Letters from the Erie Canal

Even before famine struck their homeland, some Irish were driven to emigrate by poverty. The relative prosperity they found in America is suggested in this observation by a worker on the Erie Canal, who had been hired by an illiterate coworker to write a letter to his family back in Ireland. His comments appear in *Irish Americans and Their Communities of Cleveland* by Nelson L. Callahan and William F. Hickey.

> I was writing a letter for this poor Paddy [a common term used to denote an Irish immigrant] and the Paddy wants me to tell the folks back home that he has meat three times each week. When I ask why he wanted me to write that, seeing as to how he got meat three times a day, the Paddy told me that his folks would have a hard enough time understanding him getting meat three times a week and would think he had gone daft if he told the truth.

in mosquito-ridden marshes and other low-lying areas. So high was the mortality rate on those projects that a popular saying during the nineteenth century was that one

Irish canal worker died "for each six feet of canal built."[43]

Life for canal builders was arduous. Besides the risk of death from disease and accidents, they faced foul living conditions. The laborers lived in makeshift shacks along the canals. They could have their families with them, but that did not relieve the hardship. During a visit to the United States, English novelist Charles Dickens toured an Irish labor camp, which he described this way: "Hideously ugly old women and very buxom young ones, pigs, dogs, men, children, babies, pots, kettles, dung hills, vile refuse, rank straw and standing water, all wallowing together in an inseparable heap, composed the furniture of every dark and dirty hut."[44]

For the families of the workers, the general disorder and squalor was only part of the picture. Wages were sometimes partially paid in whiskey, and in those cases the cash a worker earned was inadequate to buy enough food. Worse, the head of the household, when payday came around, might well spend his evening drinking and fighting. Brawls, in fact, were a part of life for Irish immigrant laborers, who often fought one another just for recreation.

Sickness was rampant on canal construction sites. Because canal diggers lived and worked in low-lying areas where

A group of laborers boards a train that will take them to the site of their work digging a canal.

mosquitoes bred, malaria was common. Cholera was another disease that afflicted the workers, brought on by water contaminated by human waste. Sometimes so many workers became ill that construction had to stop completely because there were too few people well enough to work.

When the workers were paid in cash, it was usually a fair wage for the times, about ten to fifteen dollars a month. But contractors often forced the workers to buy necessities at company stores, which charged exorbitant prices. And because the money to build canals and railroads came from public funds, state and local politicians could and often did hold up payments to contractors. When this happened, wages would be cut or workers would not be paid at all.

Dangerous Work

Still, there was plenty of work, if not digging canals, then building railroads. Immigrants, many of them Irish, laid thousands of miles of track across New York, Pennsylvania, Ohio, Illinois, Iowa, Georgia, and Wisconsin. The work could be dangerous because dynamite was used to carve away solid rock to make way for rails, often in precarious spots like cliff faces. In such locations, workers in straw baskets were lowered to the place to be blasted and set the charges, then they were quickly pulled up. Sometimes, though, they were caught in the explosion and killed. The death rate was so high that a popular saying of the time was that for each railroad, there was "an Irishman buried under every tie."[45]

Irish laborers work at laying track on a section of the Central Pacific Railroad.

If building railroads took a heavy toll among the Irish, even more deadly was coal mining. Miners worked long, hard hours underground. Worn down by heavy labor and the constant breathing of coal dust, they died prematurely, usually leaving wives and children without any means of supporting themselves.

The workers were expendable, and they knew it; one Irish immigrant wrote that in America, after ten or twelve years of hard labor, a worker "is of very little use afterwards—he becomes old before his time, and generally dies unheeded."[46] Particularly galling was the fact that simply feeding oneself should require risking death. As one Irish American wrote, "How often do we see such paragraphs in the paper as an Irishman drowned—an Irishman crushed by a beam—an Irishman suffocated in a pit—an Irishman blown to atoms by a steam engine, ten, twenty Irishmen buried alive by the sinking of a bank—and other like casualties in the hard toils for his daily bread?"[47]

"Cheap and Expendable"

Sometimes, the Irish found themselves given the riskiest jobs for purely economic reasons. In the South, Irish Americans performed tasks that plantation owners would not allow their slaves to do. From the plantation owner's perspective, slaves were valuable property; Irishmen, on the other hand, were, as historian Kevin Kenny writes, "cheap and expendable."[48] As a result, Irish laborers in the New Orleans area were assigned dangerous, grueling jobs, such as digging ditches in swamps teeming with snakes, alligators, and mosquitoes.

Ironically, it was precisely because the Irish took the lowest-paying jobs that most people did not want that they were ostracized by some segments of American society. For example, because of racial prejudice, free blacks working in the North were largely limited to menial jobs. When the Irish arrived and proved themselves willing to take these same jobs for lower wages, resentment was inevitable. One black man living during the 1850s wrote that the Irish were

crowding themselves into every place of business and labor, and driving the poor colored American citizen out. Along the wharves, where the colored man once done the whole business of shipping and unshipping—in stores where his services were once rendered, and in families where the chief place were filled by him, in all these situations there are substituted foreigners.[49]

Former slave and renowned abolitionist Frederick Douglass also commented on the way the Irish were taking over jobs that free blacks usually did, saying, "Every hour sees us elbowed out of some employment to make room perhaps for some newly arrived immigrants, whose hunger and color are thought to give them a title to special favor. White men are becoming house servants, cooks, stewards, common laborers and flunkeys to our gentry."[50] So great was this ill feeling that some blacks refused even to live on the same street as an Irish person.

Adding to the resentment of the Irish was that they were often used as strikebreakers,

Mother Jones: A Dangerous Woman

One Irish American who fought for better working conditions for miners was Mother Jones, considered the most dangerous woman in America by politicians in her time because of her radical views on labor. She was born Mary Harris in County Cork, Ireland, probably in 1837, and at some point during her youth she immigrated with her family to Toronto, Canada, where her father worked on the railroad. When she finished school, Harris taught for a while, then married George Jones and settled with him in Memphis, Tennessee. Mary and George had four children, but in 1867 all of the children and George died in a yellow fever epidemic. Mary, now all alone, moved to Chicago, where she became a dressmaker, working for women from some of the wealthiest families in the city. Mary was disturbed by the fact that some people were homeless and begging on the street while others, like her customers, lived in luxury. Her interest in this disparity led her to research pay rates and working conditions for those who worked at hard, low-paying jobs. As she researched, she met with representatives from the Knights of Labor, a trade organization she eventually joined. During the Chicago fire of 1871 her store and most of her possessions were burned. Jones or "Mother Jones," as she became known, turned her energies to union organization. She traveled the country making speeches for the Knights of Labor, and she helped found the International Workers of the World in 1905. Mother Jones rarely rested from what she considered her calling; when she was well into her eighties, she traveled to West Virginia to support a miners' strike, and she spent nine weeks in jail for organizing a miners' strike in Colorado in 1923. She continued to support miners and other workers until her death in 1930. In 1936 a monument to Mother Jones was erected in Minnesota. It reads, "She gave her life to the world of labor, her blessed soul to heaven. God's finger touches her, and now she sleeps."

The radical labor leader known as Mother Jones was once considered by politicians to be the most dangerous woman in America.

or "scabs," as they were known. Employers would bring them in to end a strike by other workers. Sometimes, the employers ended up keeping the Irish and firing all of those who were on strike because the Irish worked for such low pay that they saved employers a great deal of money.

Public Service

Jobs in mining, construction, and railroads were often subject to the weather—little work was done during the winter months—and the whims of the employers. City and state jobs, on the other hand, were stable and offered security and a good pension. They also did not require much in the way of education, something most of the Irish, up until the latter part of the nineteenth century, were denied, either because of poverty or discrimination. As a consequence, many Irishmen rejected the nomadic, rough-and-tumble world of canal and railroad building and mining and instead took jobs as police officers and firefighters. Like construction and mining, these jobs combined low pay with the high risk of injury or death, so they were open to the Irish.

Soon the Irish made up a substantial percentage of police officers and firefighters. In 1855, for example, 27 percent of the members of the New York City Police Department were Irish. During the 1850s in New Orleans, nearly all of the police force was Irish. San Francisco had a large contingent of Irish Americans on its police force as well: In 1848 it hired its first Irish police chief, and during the 1870s about one-third of its officers had Irish names. Thirteen of the first seventeen chiefs of the New York City Fire Department, which established a paid force in 1865, were Irish, as were seventeen of the city's first twenty-three fire commissioners. Of the one hundred firefighters killed in the line of duty between 1865 and 1905, sixty-six were Irish.

"Women's Work"

Because pay was so low and the threat of work-related injury or death so high for men, to support their families most immigrant Irishwomen also took jobs outside their homes. Many, particularly in New England, found work in factories. The "needle industries" employed many Irishwomen: In 1855 one-third of employed Irishwomen worked as seamstresses, milliners, dressmakers, shirt-collar makers, lace makers, and embroiderers. Some worked in their homes and were paid by the piece; those with small children particularly preferred this kind of work. A few Irishmen also learned to sew and became tailors. In fact, so accomplished were the men that in 1850 there were 1,547 tailors in Boston, and at least 1,000 of them were Irish.

In garment factories the Irish learned to sew both by hand and, with the invention of the sewing machine in 1846, using machines. They benefited by learning a skill, and because Irish immigrants were willing to work for such low wages, employers benefited as well. Author and historian Oscar Handlin writes that "in the two decades after 1845 the Irish energized all aspects of industrial development in Boston by holding out to investors magnificent opportunities for profits from cheap labor costs."[51]

Of course, the many immigrant Irishwomen who were single had to support themselves as well. The majority of these immigrant women became domestic servants in the United States and were employed by middle- and upper-class families in Philadelphia, New York, Boston, and other cities. These Irishwomen soon predominated in what was known simply as "service." During the 1850s, for example, about 75 percent of domestic servants in New York were Irish. The position was usually a live-in one. Sometimes domestic servants were treated as members of the family, but many were treated impersonally. Often, no matter what their given name was, these women were called by the popular Irish names "Bridget" or "Maggie," and many employers never did know their maid's real name.

Working as a servant assured a woman a place to live, but life was still hard. Domestics were expected to be available the entire day, which meant they often worked from as early as four or five A.M. to ten P.M. and sometimes later, and they were usually on their feet the entire time, cooking, ironing, mending, washing, and dusting. They earned about twenty dollars a month, and since they rarely had to pay for room or board, they could save their money. When they married, most Irish domestics resigned, although some were reluctant to do so because it meant leaving a large, comfortable

A team of Irish domestics poses on the steps of their household. The vast majority of single Irishwomen who immigrated took work as servants.

Nellie Bly

Not all Irish American women worked as servants or factory workers. One woman of Irish American heritage became one of the most popular journalists of her time. Nellie Bly was born Elizabeth Jane Cochran. One day, when she was in her late teens, Elizabeth read an editorial in the *Pittsburgh Dispatch* that argued that women should not work outside the home. Angered, Elizabeth wrote a letter to the newspaper. The editor liked the spirit of the letter and offered her a job as a reporter, with the pen name "Nellie Bly."

Bly began to write articles about the poor and downtrodden. Her first story was about the lives of working girls; she found a job working in a sweatshop, then wrote about the poor conditions there. After her story appeared, factory owners threatened to withdraw their advertising from the newspaper, so Bly's editors told her she could only write about fashion and flower shows on the women's page. She did that for a while, then persuaded her editor to let her become a foreign correspondent in Mexico for six months. When she returned, though, they put her back on the women's page.

Frustrated by what appeared to be her editor's lack of support for her because she was a woman, Bly quit and went to New York to find work. After four months she was assigned by an important newspaper, the *New York World,* to do a story on the mentally ill in New York. Bly surprised the editor by actually posing as a mentally ill woman and getting into Blackwell's Island, a mental institution. She spent ten days there, then wrote about her experiences. What she uncovered—beatings, force-feedings, cold baths—resulted in reform at the institution. Bly continued to pioneer the field of investigative reporting. In 1889 she became famous for an around-the-world trip that took seventy-two days; she was trying to beat the time it took the main character of a popular novel of the time, *Around the World in Eighty Days* by Jules Verne, and she was successful. On her return, she was greeted by a cheering crowd and fireworks. Later, Bly married a wealthy businessman, Robert Seaman. When he died, she attempted to run his businesses, but her skills as a businesswoman were not as good as her talents as a journalist, and the businesses failed. Bly then returned to journalism. She died in 1922 at the age of 64.

house to live in a tenement apartment. In addition, married women had to rely on their husband's wages rather than earn their own, and they had to ask their husbands for money when they wanted something.

Some women deliberately chose to work in a factory rather than in a private home as a servant. At least, they said, factory hours were regular—usually about ten hours a day—and one's privacy was respected. One female factory worker who made boxes all day said, "Our day is ten hours long, but when it's done it's done, and we can do what we like with the evenings. That's what I've heard from every nice girl who ever tried [domestic] service. You're never sure that your soul's your own except when you are out of the house, and I couldn't stand that a day."[52] Although that worker seemed happy with her life, it was not without its difficulties. Many Irishwomen who worked in factories lived in nearby boardinghouses that were crowded and noisy. At work they were on their feet all day, usually in large rooms filled with noisy machines.

The fact that Irishwomen had to work caused many in established society—the very group who oppressed Irish immigrants—to look down on them. In those days, it was believed that married women, with or without children, should stay home and be homemakers. Many Irishwomen would have liked to have had that option. Most did not.

"No Irish Need Apply"

The Irish found many jobs in labor and service, but they were sometimes subject to blatant discrimination. Newspaper advertisements announcing job openings sometimes openly excluded Irish people from applying for a job. An advertisement in the September 4, 1830, edition of the *New York Evening Post* announced this: "WANTED. A Cook or a Chambermaid. They must be American, Scotch, Swiss, or Africans—no Irish."[53] Signs also appeared in storefronts or business windows that read "No Irish Need Apply."

There were several reasons Americans discriminated against the Irish. These new arrivals were Catholic, first of all, and until the tide of Irish immigrants flowed into the United States, the country was primarily made up of Protestants, many of whom harbored suspicions about a faith they knew nothing about. Some potential employers even believed that an Irish Catholic maid living in their home could somehow be a spy for the pope. Some employers were also reluctant to hire Irish workers because they saw them as dirty or lazy. Moreover, many Irish immigrants drank heavily; the group as a whole had a disproportionately high level of alcoholism, and the Irish were notorious for public drunkenness, which did not endear them to established citizens.

The Irish did have some advantages over many other immigrants at the time. For one thing, they spoke English, and many employers hired them because they could easily communicate with them. Moreover, they were willing to do almost any job. They also presented a cheerful demeanor, particularly Irishwomen, who were known to be loyal servants who were grateful to work in the homes of the wealthy.

Farmers

Although most of the Irish who immigrated to the United States during the mid-1800s were from rural areas, when they arrived, they settled in cities and found work there. A few, however—about 15 percent—turned to farming. Some, finding that jobs in mining they had been told of did not exist, took work as farm laborers instead; others simply stayed on wherever they were after their jobs building railroads or canals were finished and took jobs as farmhands, blacksmiths, or store clerks. Farmwork seemed to be satisfying for some immigrants. During the 1850s, for example, farm laborer Andrew Greenlees wrote to his brother in Ireland from Plattsburgh, New York, saying, "In this country Jack's as good as his master, if he don't like one then go to another, plenty of work and plenty of wages, plenty to eat and no landlords, that's enough, what more does a man want?"[54]

Meanwhile, news had spread in Ireland of good farmland being available in America. For example, one Irish landowner said in 1849 that one of his tenants had just returned from a visit to the United States, and "he assured me that for 600 miles along the banks of the Mississippi (and he is a very respectable man) he had traversed the vast tracts of land, the worst of which was better than the best acre I have in the world, and I have some of the very best in Ireland."[55] By 1850 there were thousands of Irish farmers scattered throughout the Midwest.

Workers Uniting

Whatever the job, however, the Irish were often expected to accept poor treatment at the hands of their employer. Not surprisingly,

A high rate of alcoholism led Irish Americans to be stereotyped as drunks, as in this sketch from the 1870s.

in such an environment, labor strife was common. For example, in 1853 in La Salle, Illinois, laborers building a bridge over the Illinois River were told that wages would be cut from $1.25 to $1.00 a day. Many workers, including a large Irish contingent, went on strike. The work soon resumed, but on payday, while wages were being distributed, an accounting error was discovered and the payment process was halted. An angry mob then ran to the contractor's office, and the frightened contractor shot and killed one of the laborers. The mob then beat the contractor to death.

This was neither the first nor the last such confrontation between laborers and contractors. Indeed, Irish laborers became known for resorting to violence to make their grievances known. As professor and historian Kevin Kenny writes, "The unskilled Irish . . . had available to them a rich tradition of violent resistance in rural Ireland, which they deployed to dramatic effect along the canals, public works and railroads of early industrial America."[56] Sometimes, when wages were not paid, Irish workers would in protest destroy the work they had completed. One renowned group of Irish protestors called themselves the Molly Maguires. Several of its members were convicted of murder and were executed.

Besides fighting with employers, the Irish also fought among themselves for jobs, former residents of one Irish county against those from another county. For example, in Huntington, Indiana, hundreds of Irish laborers engaged in a feud and divided into factions of workers from Cork County, Ireland, and workers from Ulster, now in Northern Ireland, and prepared for battle. They had to be separated by members of a militia, who were called in as the two groups prepared to fight.

As more Irish came to America, secret societies sprang up to address some of their needs. The idea for these societies had begun in Ireland hundreds of years earlier; many of them were formed to protect priests and their parishioners in response to anti-Catholic laws that were inflicted upon the Irish by the English. In the United States, membership in the societies was often based on what part of Ireland one came from. Members had secret handshakes,

John L. Sullivan

John L. Sullivan was an idol for many Irishmen, young and old, during the late nineteenth century because he was among the first Irish Americans to rise to the level of champion in American sports. His success in boxing gave the Irish American community a reason to cheer.

Sullivan was born in Boston and lived in a tenement. In 1877 he attended a boxing match, and when a local fighter offered to take on spectators, Sullivan stepped forward. Sullivan knocked him out, and that was the start of a fifteen-year career in boxing. Sullivan was boastful and brash, which made audiences love him even more, and he seemed fearless: One fight in 1889, a bout for the heavyweight title, lasted for seventy-five rounds before his opponent collapsed in exhaustion. Sullivan was the heavyweight champion for ten years but spent much of his winnings on alcohol and gradually became overweight and out of shape. He lost his title in 1892, when he was thirty-four, to "Gentleman" Jim Corbett, a younger Irish boxer. Sullivan then toured the world, sometimes acting in plays and giving exhibition fights. In 1908 he married his childhood sweetheart and stopped drinking—he even gave speeches encouraging temperance. He and his wife bought a farm in Massachusetts, where he lived until his death in 1918.

passwords, and other gestures, and they protected one another's rights to work on a particular job. They also protested poor working conditions and sometimes resorted to violence to make their point when they felt they had no other choice.

As time went on, however, Irish workers learned to use strikes to force their employers to treat them fairly. For example, in 1853 Irish workers struck the Erie Railroad, successfully demanding a ten-hour workday and a $1.25-per-day wage. By 1910, there were 110 member unions in the American Federation of Labor, and almost half of them were led by Irish Americans.

Inflicting Prejudice

Just as they experienced discrimination, some Irish practiced it themselves, and labor unions were also used to bar other ethnic groups from jobs the Irish wanted. Not only did Irish workers attempt to block blacks from taking their jobs, but the Chinese were also victims of their labor practices. This was especially true in California during the 1870s, when Chinese immigrants were beginning to look for work building railroads there. These new workers were willing to take jobs at pay rates lower than those the Irish had fought for and won. The Irish protested against the hiring of Chinese workers, but these demonstrations were about more than just jobs. Kevin Kenny writes that the Irish were using their protests against Chinese workers as a means of assimilation: "The presence of a new alien minority [gave] the Irish yet another opportunity to protest and demonstrate their fitness for inclusion in the racial mainstream."[57] Although the Irish

The Molly Maguires

Hundreds of Irishmen labored in the anthracite coal mines of western Pennsylvania during the 1800s. One secretive organization of Irish American laborers called itself the Molly Maguires; about three thousand Irish workers were members. The Molly Maguires operated out of saloons, and saloon keepers, many of them former miners, were its leaders. Law enforcement officers believed that the Molly Maguires were responsible for about fifty murders in Schuylkill County, Pennsylvania, alone, and based on their findings the members of the Molly Maguires were arrested and charged with murder. Twenty members were convicted and executed; the remaining men were sent to prison. The Catholic Church denounced the Molly Maguires and expressed its fears that the group reinforced the stereotype that many Americans had of the Irish as violent bullies.

had been and still were victims of discrimination themselves, they seemed to think it necessary to inflict that same sort of bias on another group. In fact, in 1882 a federal law was passed outlawing further immigration of Chinese workers, a result of pressure from the primarily Irish labor movement.

The cover of an 1878 edition of the humor magazine Puck *features an unflattering depiction of Irish and Chinese immigrants arriving in the United States.*

Success in the Workplace

Over time, as Irish Americans proved that they were hardworking and dependable, the old stereotypes faded. Gradually, too, the mutual suspicion that had fed anti-Catholic—and, by extension, anti-Irish—prejudice gave way to a measure of respect and tolerance, opening additional opportunities for the Irish and their American-born children and grandchildren. Professions such as teaching and nursing became strongholds for Irish Americans, to the point that by 1870 about one-fifth of all schoolteachers in New York City were Irishwomen, and by 1910 about one-third of Chicago's teachers were of Irish descent. Men made gains in the workplace as well. Decades of building railroads and working on other major projects had afforded Irish immigrants the experience they needed to open their own contracting and construction companies. As early as the 1870s, about 20 percent of building contractors in the United States were Irish. Sticking together, these contractors largely hired from within their own community. This meant that more and more Irish could find work.

But although first- and second-generation Irish Americans began to work at skilled jobs or even to own their own companies, most historians concede that their ascendancy occurred primarily within the Irish community. According to Kenny, "Irish social mobility typically occurred within the working class, from unskilled to semi-skilled or skilled labor."[58] A new generation would soon apply the lessons learned in organizing labor unions to organizing and wielding political power. Irish Americans were ready to take control not just of their own destiny but also that of the entire nation.

CHAPTER FIVE

The Irish and Politics

A s the number of Irish Americans grew, they soon were able to wield considerable political influence. Yet that clout was not easily gained. Just as some other Americans had hesitated to hire Irish workers, some old-line politicians worked aggressively to stop Irish Americans from gaining political power.

Resisting Reform

These politicians harnessed the resentment many Americans felt toward Irish immigrants—resentment born of Irish resistance to a number of popular social reforms. Historian Oscar Handlin writes that the Irish saw reform as "a delusion inflating man's

sense of importance, distorting the relative significance of earthly values and obscuring the true goals of their endeavour—their eternal souls." Their resistance, he goes on to write, could also be the result of their living for so long under "enforced obedience," which had made them resigned to the idea that things should remain as they had always been.[59]

One reform that most Irish opposed was the abolition of slavery. Many Irish followed the Catholic Church's teachings on slavery at the time: Abuse of slaves was wrong, but slavery in itself was not inherently wrong. Irish Americans also had practical reasons for opposing the abolition of slavery: They would have to compete for jobs with the newly freed blacks who would be leaving the plantations.

At the same time, the tendency of Irish Catholics to send their children to parochial schools aroused resentment among those who were pressing for publicly supported education. Some politicians fueled this resentment by promoting the idea that Irish Catholics thought American schools were not good enough for their children.

Further fueling anti-Irish sentiment was the refusal of many Irish to support the movement to ban the sale of alcoholic beverages. Some Irish Americans did join the temperance movement, forming the Catholic Sons of Temperance, and some Catholic priests encouraged their congregations to stop drinking, but on the whole, Irish Americans did not support the movement. Anti-Irish politicians used as ammunition the fact that the Irish represented a large percentage of those arrested for public drunkenness.

The Anti-Catholic Movement

The antipathy of Irish immigrants to reforms such as abolition, public education, and temperance played into the hands of nativists—individuals who believed that immigrants were somehow threatening to take over the United States. Many nativists focused on the Catholicism of the Irish as well as other immigrants and formed secretive organizations whose goals were to prevent Catholics from gaining political and social influence in the United States.

Among these were the American Protective Association, the Guardians of Liberty, and the American Minute Men.

Publications such as *America: The Journal for Americans,* which espoused extreme anti-Catholic views, also began to show up around the country. Every week for more than three years, this journal warned Americans about the intentions of the Catholic Church in America. Novels with veiled anti-Catholic themes were published as well. Some of these promoted the notion that a maid would try to convert the children of her Protestant employer to Catholicism or would spirit them away to church and have them baptized as Catholics.

For their part, Irish Catholics harbored suspicions of Protestants in America. Irish-run publications did not help to mend the rift between Catholics and the Protestant majority. For example, in the July 29, 1859, edition of *Boston Pilot,* an editor wrote that "cooperation for any length of time in important matters between true Catholics and real Protestants is morally impossible."[60]

The Know-Nothing Party

An outgrowth of the nativist movement and its anti-Catholic stance was the American Party. Also called the Know-Nothings because members were instructed to say, when questioned, that they knew nothing about it, the party tried to stop Irish Catholics from gaining political power by proposing laws that would have required immigrants to live in the United States for

Members of the Know-Nothings attend a torchlight meeting in New York City. This secretive party was staunchly anti-Catholic and worked to prevent Irish Americans from gaining political power.

more than twenty years before they could become citizens.

For a while, the Know-Nothings enjoyed political success. In 1854, for example, the Know-Nothing candidate won almost 40 percent of the vote for governor in Pennsylvania. That same year, the party took control of the Massachusetts state legislature, and the state's governor was a Know-Nothing as well, as was the mayor of Boston. Those numbers indicate just how powerful anti-Irish and anti-Catholic feelings were in Massachusetts, especially in Boston, where many Irish immigrants

settled. That Boston's political and social leaders should harbor such resentment of the Irish was consistent with their strong cultural ties to the British, who traditionally viewed the Irish as inferior. The elites of Boston felt that their city had been invaded by the Irish, whom they considered to be drunken and unruly. As a result of this anti-Irish sentiment, in 1854 two out of three voters in Massachusetts voted for Know-Nothing candidates.

After the Know-Nothings were elected to the Massachusetts legislature, they passed legislation targeting the state's Irish

Catholics. For example, one law made mandatory the reading of the King James Bible in public schools. The Irish lacked the power to defeat such laws, but events were soon to give the Irish American the chance to overcome prejudice and discrimination.

The Irish in the Civil War

The claims by the nativists and Know-Nothings that the Irish were somehow disloyal were finally laid to rest with the outbreak of the Civil War. Although the Irish had little interest in seeing slavery end in the United States, many had, by the 1860s, become American citizens and felt a personal stake in restoring the unity of their adopted land. Of the part Irish Americans played in the Civil War, historian Thomas N. Brown writes that, "By sharing in its agonies, for whatever the reason and however much against their will, the Irish participated intimately in the American people's most terrible experience."[61]

Although hundreds of Irish fought for the Confederacy, at least 144,000 Irish American soldiers joined the Union army. Irish soldiers fought bravely in many battles. During the Battle of Fredericksburg, for

St. Patrick's Battalion

From 1846 to 1848, the United States warred with Mexico over territory that both countries claimed in Texas. During the war, one group of men deserted the U.S. army in 1846 and fought on the side of Mexico. Called St. Patrick's Battalion, or, in Spanish, El Batallon de San Patricio, this force primarily comprised Irish American soldiers. Their reasons for fleeing to Mexico were several; most historians agree that the primary reason was that they were angered at the barbaric way the Protestant American soldiers treated Mexican Catholic priests and nuns. Because they were Catholic, the Irish soldiers also complained that they were treated badly by American soldiers. Irish-born John Riley claimed that he organized St.

Patrick's Battalion. At first there were about forty-eight men in the company, but the numbers grew to more than two thousand by July 1847. The battalion hoisted a green silk banner as it prepared for battle; on one side of the banner was an image of St. Patrick and on the other side, a shamrock and a harp. It was said that Mexican nuns sewed the banner.

From May 1846 to August 1847 the battalion fought with the Mexican army. During the last battle, about eighty of the Irish deserters were captured and were either executed or punished by branding. Whereas they were considered traitors by the U.S. army, in Mexico the members of the San Patricios were considered heroes, and they are still honored as such today.

example, many of those injured or killed were Irish, and one large Irish regiment from New York City, the Fighting Sixtyninth, was renowned for its heroism. The Civil War, in fact, did much to help the Irish begin to identify themselves as Americans. One historian notes that, during the Civil War, Irish Americans "lost the sense of inferiority and acquired the sense of belonging."[62]

A Civil War–era recruiting poster urges Irish Americans to join the Union army. Loyal to their adopted land, Irish Americans enlisted on the side of the Union in large numbers.

The Civil War also provided to many Irish Americans motivation to try to eliminate some fundamental inequities in their adopted country. The draft system of the time provided men who were well-off the option of paying another man three hundred dollars to fight in their stead. Most Irish Americans, however, did not have that kind of money, and so they went off to fight and die while wealthier men remained at home. The unfairness of this system frustrated and angered Irish Americans and aroused in them the determination to use their growing numbers to elect politicians who would represent their interests at the local, state, and national levels.

The Irish Gain Power

After the Civil War, Irish Americans, with their newfound sense of belonging and their powerful voting bloc, began to make real political gains in the United States. Historians agree that the Irish seemed to combine a natural affinity for politics with an instinctive understanding of the way the American government operated. One remarked, for example, that "the Irish were natural politicians—warm, witty and gregarious, flexible and practical, energetic and aggressive. To the American political scene they brought the advantages of numbers and strong clan loyalties, fluency in the language, and an understanding of the Anglo-Saxon constitutional tradition."[63] Moreover, political participation was a good way of guaranteeing their own future. As historian Kevin Kenny writes, "The Irish began to discover in politics not only a means of protection from nativist attack but a potential path to power for themselves."[64] Having been oppressed in Ireland and similarly so during their early years in America, by the 1850s the Irish were ready to participate in government as they never had before.

The fact that the Irish tended to settle in close-knit communities in American cities worked to their advantage when it came to politics. Irish American politicians saw the difficulties unique to city living in immigrant neighborhoods—indeed, most of them had firsthand experience living in such conditions—and as a result worked to make life easier for voters. This very local, grassroots approach to governing grew in many cities to encompass the entire political apparatus.

The "Machine"

The Irish used politics probably more than any other means to achieve success. Because the particular form of government developed by Irish politicians in New York worked so efficiently to elect chosen candidates, it became known as a political machine. Leaders in other cities, such as San Francisco and Chicago, began to implement machine politics as well, and by the 1890s political machines dominated by Irish politicians led several large U.S. cities.

Machine politicians were not as concerned with democratic principles as they were with more practical issues, and they used government as a means of gaining and distributing power. Those involved in the machine used a system in which favors were granted in return for votes. The machine relied on operatives from the highest official in the city down to block captains,

William "Boss" Tweed of New York was a master of machine politics, a system developed by Irish American politicians for controlling local elections.

who were responsible for a city block. Block residents would visit their captain, who was often the local saloon keeper, to ask for help in getting a job or some other kind of assistance. The captain would grant the favor if he could, or he would go to the next highest official, the precinct captain, who would do what he could or go to the ward boss above him. If a family's main wage earner was injured or died, for example, the machine saw to it that the family was taken care of financially by paying its rent and other bills and making sure the family had food and other necessities.

Political operatives could see to it that virtually anyone who asked for a job received one, either working directly for the city or for one of the many companies that did business with the city. These people might not get the exact job that they hoped to get, but if they voted for the machine's candidate, they would get a job. Writer Marjorie R. Fallows explains that this arrangement was "a patronage system that would bind politician and constituent together in a web of mutual obligation and loyalty."[65] The system resulted in the elimination of the anti-Catholic discrimination that had existed during the nineteenth century.

Because machine politicians were able to achieve results that private citizens often could not, residents of Irish neighborhoods revered and respected them and actually expected little in the way of material compensation. Often a precinct captain, simply by attending the funeral of a constituent's relative or simply with the tip of his hat, could assure ongoing political support for his boss.

For all that machine politicians achieved, such a system had its dark side. When a machine politician decided that favors were insufficient to gain support, he often resorted to intimidation by local street gangs. For example, in lower Manhattan, where most Irish Americans in New York lived, local gangs such as the Dead Rabbits, the Forty Thieves, the Plug Uglies, and the Roach Guards made certain that people voted the way the city's Irish mayor wanted. Even the volunteer fire departments, whose members were mostly Irish Americans, would sometimes engage in political intimidation.

Other times, a machine politician would simply pay people to vote his way, or he would register people to vote who had died or moved away, then cast their votes in his favor. Ballots cast for an opponent might be stolen and destroyed before they could be counted, or members of the police force, who were predominantly Irish, might stop people from going to the polls if they knew those people planned to vote for their opponents. It was not unheard of for machine "bosses" to recruit voters from saloons and march them to the polls with the promise of free liquor in return for votes. For all the considerable good a politician might intend, historian Ann Kathleen Bradley identified the primary goal of machine politicians as "winning power and then keeping it, and they tolerated and even encouraged corruption and graft, subservience and hypocrisy."[66]

Reformers, who had long bemoaned the antipathy of the Irish toward social change, denounced political machines as immoral. Machine politicians were actually practicing a kind of practical reform, though, in their battle with the anti-Irish, anti-Catholic prejudice they had been experiencing for decades. Lawrence J. McCaffrey writes of Irish politicians that their "conservative, skeptical, often cynical attitude toward man and his environment has made the Irish more successful as practical reformers than ideological liberals have been."[67]

Nationalism

At the same time that they were harnessing political power to help themselves in

America, Irish Americans were also banding together to further the cause of a free Ireland. Some of the groups wanted what was called home rule—an Irish parliament separate from England's. Others wanted complete freedom from British rule.

Whatever the long-range goal, the cause of Irish nationalism was a popular one among Irish Americans during the nineteenth century. The largest group working for Irish independence was called the Fenian Brotherhood, which began in New York City in 1858. By 1860 the Fenian Brotherhood had spread across the country, and most cities with an Irish population had a Fenian group. By the late 1870s, the Fenians boasted ten thousand members. Many were Civil War veterans who wanted to use their newly acquired military skills in the fight for Ireland's freedom.

After factional disagreements eroded the unity of the Fenians, another group formed, called Clan na Gael (Children of the Gael), which also supported the cause of a free Ireland. Founded in 1867, the society was known secretly as the United Brotherhood. The group hoped to achieve Irish independence by supplying arms for Ireland in preparation for a rebellion against Britain. During the 1880s Clan na Gael weakened, but it regained some of its strength during the early 1900s with new leadership. The newly revitalized organization wanted more than just a separate parliament for Ireland: It advocated complete independence.

Another group, the United Irish League of America (UILA), was founded in the United States in 1901 and soon had two hundred branches. Most of its members were professionals who had more money than did the primarily working-class members of Clan na Gael. The UILA contributed money and effort toward an autonomous Irish parliament. In 1919 another group formed, the American Association for the Recognition of the Irish Republic, and it soon had 750,000 members.

Members of nationalistic organizations provided more than just support for the nationalist cause. Resistance leaders still in Ireland saw Irish Americans, who were gradually achieving a measure of prosperity, as being able to provide inexhaustible funds toward the movement. Historian Matthew Fry Jacobson says Irish America was "an incalculable bankroll for political projects, ranging from land reform to violent overthrow."[68] More than twelve hundred local chapters of the Irish Land League of America reacted to the Land War in Ireland, which was a series of armed uprisings by dispossessed Irishmen that occurred from 1879 to 1882, by collecting several hundred thousand dollars and sending the sum to Ireland, and it has been estimated that private donations from Americans during the Land War were more than $5 million.

Affecting Foreign Policy

The intense sympathy felt by Irish Americans for their motherland also affected U.S. foreign policy. State legislatures, pressured by their many Irish American voters, whose votes they were anxious to keep, passed resolutions condemning the actions of the British in Ireland during the Land War. Some Irish Americans even returned to Ireland to support the rebellion and were

The Fenians Invade Canada

In the spring of 1866, the Fenian Brotherhood formulated a plot to invade Canada, which at the time was a British territory. The plan was to capture Canada and hold it hostage until Ireland gained its independence from Britain. In March of that year, the Fenian Brotherhood held a rally in New York City, and one hundred thousand Irish Americans attended. On April 10, heartened by the rally and certain they had sufficient support and arms, the Fenians began their first invasion. A group of them gathered at Eastport, Maine, with the intention of invading Canada's nearby Campobello Island. But as they approached, they were met by British warships and Canadian militia, and gave up as a result.

The next invasion was planned for May 31, and it was much more successful. A group of about 800 Fenians, led by John O'Neill, who had been a captain in the Civil War, crossed the Niagara River at Buffalo, New York. They captured a British settlement, Fort Erie, where they cut telegraph lines to prevent communication between the British there and forces stationed elsewhere. The Fenians then proceeded inland to Ridgeway, Ontario, where they battled Canadian forces. But by June 3, the Canadians had managed to muster 20,000 men, so the Fenians retreated across the Niagara River, into the United States.

The third invasion occurred on June 7. About 1,000 Fenians crossed into Quebec from Vermont. However, when United States. authorities seized supplies they had stored on the American side of the border, the Fenians were forced to retreat.

The Fenians made one final attempt to invade Canada nearly four years later, on Queen Victoria's birthday, May 24, 1870. Again, the Canadians were ready, and they forced the Irish American troops back over the border. This time, O'Neill was arrested by jailed as a result by the British. Their plight drew national attention, and the U.S. government was forced to get involved, negotiating with the British to free these Irish American citizens.

Irish Americans were better able to raise money and draw attention to the plight of the Irish in the United States than they had been when they lived in Ireland. As historian Carl Wittke notes, "British policy had pushed the Irishman westward across the ocean only to produce a new and more powerful Ireland in the free air of America."[69] But Irish Americans found that solidarity over nationalism was difficult to achieve. Historian Thomas N. Brown attributes the difficulty to the fact that "the immigrant community too closely reflected

American authorities and charged with violating neutrality laws. With the invasion of Canada a clear failure, many members of the Fenian Brotherhood gave up, and the organization quietly dwindled away.

In expectation of a raid by the Fenian Brotherhood, Canadian soldiers guard a suspension bridge.

the divisions of class and section within American life, and personal and organizational jealousies were too intense."[70] Most Irish Americans supported Irish nationalism, but many disagreed about how best to achieve it. Some factions advocated violence, but others did not, believing that more conservative tactics, such as withholding rent payments to landlords, would be effective in achieving the political reforms they sought for Ireland.

Still, an Irish uprising on Easter weekend in 1916 was supported by most Irish Americans who advocated a free Ireland. Much of the support and leadership for the rebellion came from Clan na Gael, and many other organizations and individuals supported the cause as well. In fact, as

Soldiers and civilians engage in combat on a smoke-filled Dublin street during the 1916 Easter Uprising, a rebellion that most Irish Americans supported.

armed rebellion spread across Ireland between 1916 and 1921, Irish Americans raised about $10 million for the cause of Irish independence.

Irish American Journalists and Politics

Publications run by Irish Americans highlighted nationalist issues and kept the hope for a free Ireland in the forefront. Even before the Irish began to take political control of many American cities, Irish American journalists were wielding power through the written word. The *Boston Pilot,* an Irish-run newspaper, had been an influential publication even before Fenian leader John Boyle O'Reilly became its editor in 1875. O'Reilly focused much of his attention on issues of Irish nationalism. Patrick Ford, editor of the New York newspaper *Irish World,* also used his publication as a forum for his views. He echoed the beliefs of the Irish Land League, for example, when he proclaimed that all land belonged to God and, by extension, to his people, and that men should not profit from renting out land. These publications and others like them exhorted Irish Americans to support the cause of nationalism. The *Irish World,* for example, asked readers to "keep alive the flames of patriotism which will light to her final deliverance our motherland."[71]

Irish and Democrat

Irish American voters backed those who would take their concerns seriously, but historically Irish American politicians were Democrats. Historian Wittke states that the very word *democrat* held appeal for the Irish, "for it was democracy that attracted them to immigrate to the United States."[72] Prior to the Civil War, the Republican backing of abolition of slavery had repelled many Irish from that party. Although Republicans often tried to win over the Irish, because the political machine stressed party loyalty above almost all other values, most Irish in America were expected to vote for Democrats.

Moreover, by its very nature, the Democratic Party's contention that the government had a legitimate role in people's lives rang true with the Irish. One historian writes that Irish machine politicians were successful because of "their willingness to

Alfred E. Smith

An Irish American named Alfred E. Smith was the first Catholic to be nominated for president of the United States. His grandparents emigrated from Ireland to the United States in 1841. Smith was born in the Lower East Side of Manhattan in 1873 and spent his childhood in a tenement apartment under the Brooklyn Bridge. Smith's father died when he was in the eighth grade, so he quit school to go work. He held several jobs, including one at the Fulton Fish Market, until a politically connected friend found a job for him as a clerk in a county office. Smith became interested in politics, and over the next fifteen years he held such offices as assemblyman, sheriff of New York County, and finally state governor. In 1928 he was nominated to run as the Democratic candidate for president against Herbert Hoover. Hoover won, and an Irish Catholic did not become president until John F. Kennedy won the office in 1960.

Alfred Smith, the first Catholic to be nominated for president of the United States, delivers a campaign speech on CBS radio.

meet the basic needs of the city's rank and file, which were ignored by Whig [forerunner of the Republican Party] politicians, who believed 'the best government is the one which governs least.'"[73] Policies advocated by the Democrats went to the heart of what mattered most to Irish Americans: jobs, security, a place to live, and food to eat. Thanks to consistent support from Irish American voters, Democrats controlled the political scene in cities across America, from New York and Boston to Chicago and San Francisco. In Boston, for example, all six of the city's mayors from 1903 to 1945 were Irish Americans.

Entering National Politics

Yet for all their success in running for local and state political office, Irish Americans had yet to succeed at the national level. Alfred E. Smith, the son of Irish immigrants, had risen through the political ranks to be elected New York's governor, and in 1928 he ran for president, only to be defeated by Herbert Hoover. Many historians believe the primary reason he lost was lingering religious intolerance.

It would, in fact, be more than three decades before Americans would vote for a Catholic as president. And even as he campaigned, John F. Kennedy would be forced to publicly distance himself from his faith. In a 1960 speech, Kennedy said, "I do not speak for my church on public matters—and the church does not speak for me."[74] Kennedy's election to the nation's highest office was the affirmation, not just that a Catholic could be elected but also that Irish Americans had entered the nation's political and social mainstream.

As Kennedy's election would later prove, Irish Americans overcame great prejudice as they fought to gain power in the United States. Yet in early decades of the twentieth century, prejudice against them, in part because of their faith, would be a problem. Irish Americans were becoming accepted in political circles, but there remained, especially among America's social elite, a reluctance to include Catholics in general and Irish Catholics in particular. As one historian, Thomas N. Brown, remarks, "They could run the cities, but they could not get into the country clubs."[75] As the realization spread that the Irish could contribute more than just toil and sweat to the country, Irish Americans began to find that their efforts to be accepted were beginning to be rewarded.

CHAPTER SIX

Respectability and Assimilation

In their effort to find acceptance in American society, the Irish had to overcome several roadblocks, including negative stereotypes and suspicions about their loyalty. As they attempted to surmount these obstacles, however, Irish Americans traded away some of the very things that made them Irish.

Fighting Stereotypes

At the turn of the twentieth century, Irish Americans were firmly established economically, but some negative stereotypes remained—often perpetuated by plays and novels popular at the time. On stage, Irish Americans, particularly men, were portrayed as buffoons—stupid but likeable drunks who wore rags, lived in slums, and got into all sorts of predicaments because of their dim-wittedness. The characters were often nicknamed "Mick" or "Paddy," both derogatory names for Irishmen.

Even the economic success that Irish Americans were now enjoying was mocked. For example, Irish actor Ned Harrigan played the part of a character named Dan Mulligan, who progressed from an unschooled immigrant right off the boat to find success as a saloon keeper and went on to become a wealthy businessman living on Madison Avenue in Manhattan. Even in his fine home, though, Mulligan was a buffoon, behaving in a manner inappropriate for elite society.

Performances like Harrigan's were initially popular with working-class Irish Americans, who identified with Mulligan's naïveté and lack of social graces. Eventually, however, Irish Americans began to object vociferously to such depictions. In 1907, for example, a group of Irish Americans went to a show in New York that featured the Russell brothers—Irish American actors who dressed up as maids who drank on the job and acted foolishly. At that performance, the audience pelted the actors with eggs, potatoes, and even rocks, forcing them offstage to a chorus of boos. The Russells had to leave New York City and were forced to abandon their act altogether.

Irish Americans also began to protest the way they were portrayed in print. Some cartoonists, for instance, consistently portrayed the Irish as apelike, with a shillelagh (a type of walking stick) in one hand and a bottle of whiskey in the other. The cartoons of Thomas Nast, whose work was widely published during the second half of the nineteenth century, particularly offended Irish Americans. Nast depicted Irishmen with monkey faces, his way of suggesting that they were somehow subhuman. Nast also promoted the idea that Irish Catholics were somehow a threat to the United States by depicting a crocodile, which he labeled the Catholic Church, crawling ashore.

As part of their efforts to overcome negative stereotypes, Irish Americans began to focus on the positive aspects of their culture and formed organizations whose purposes were to bolster that culture. These groups included the American Irish Historic

Gaelic: A Dying Language?

In sixteenth-century Ireland, most of the people spoke Gaelic, which is usually called Irish, but under the harsh rule of the English the Irish language began to die out. Yet at the time of the famine, as many as 4 million people still spoke Irish, and quite a few people in Ireland spoke English and used some Irish phrases. The number of Irish-speaking people was significantly reduced by the end of the nineteenth century, to just under 700,000, and by the time first- and second-generation Irish Americans were born, Gaelic was practically nonexistent among Irish Americans. Today, with resurgence of interest in Irish culture in both nations, classes in Irish are taught in Ireland as well as in the United States.

Society, established in 1897, which kept track of the Irish in America, and the New York Society for the Preservation of the Irish Language. This latter organization promoted the use of Gaelic, or Irish, language. Literary societies also formed to study Irish as well as other kinds of literature. New York had the Irving and Moore Literary Association and the Cosmopolitan Literary Club. In Washington, D.C., Irish

Americans socialized and discussed literature at the Thomas Davis Club, and Hartford, Connecticut, had the Hibernian Institute for those interested in reading and literature. Many other Irish literary societies existed throughout the country, as did debating societies. Although some of the meetings of these organizations were well attended, many were not, and most died out as the cohesive Irish American community began to disintegrate during the twentieth century.

Proving Their Loyalty

Despite their efforts to gain acceptance, just as earlier generations had to do during the Civil War, Irish Americans during the twentieth century had to prove their loyalty during wartime. World War I broke out in 1914, with Germany and its allies fighting against Britain, France, Russia, and their allies. The United States, not wishing to get involved in European conflicts, remained neutral for several years but finally entered the war in 1917, on the side of the British.

It was difficult for some Irish Americans to agree with this alliance. Some hoped that Britain would lose the war, thereby affording Ireland a chance to break away and become an independent republic. Even those who were comfortable with the alliance resented the British, who they felt had persecuted and repressed the Irish for years. Ultimately, the Irish Americans wholeheartedly joined in supporting the Allies in World War I, and when the United States entered the war, Irish American soldiers fought heroically.

A statue of Irish-born John Barry, hero of the American Revolutionary War, stands in Philadelphia's Independence Square.

Divided Loyalties

In the early decades of the twentieth century the idea that some immigrants might have divided loyalties did not seem far-fetched. As World War I was just beginning, U.S. president Woodrow Wilson suggested that the Irish—or any other immigrant group—might harbor some feeling for the old country. At the dedication of a monument to the Revolutionary War commodore John Barry, Wilson noted that some Americans still "need hyphens in their names because only part of them has come over."[76] Many construed the statement as questioning the patriotism of foreign-born Americans, and immigrants all over the country, including the Irish, were offended. They wondered whether Wilson was referring to them directly and to their efforts to gain independence for Ireland from Britain.

After the war ended in 1918, many Irish American veterans felt betrayed not only by the fact that Wilson continued to comment on "hyphenated Americans" but also by the fact that he seemed to show no interest in Ireland. They urged politicians to support Ireland's fight for freedom, often likening its plight to that of America just before the American Revolution. The apathy of Wilson, a Democrat, resulted in some Irish Americans turning away from the party they had so long supported.

Even after Irish Americans had bravely fought in World War I, many of them placed such a great emphasis on the problems in Ireland that other Americans wondered just how loyal they were to the United States. Their hearts seemed divided between their mother country and the country they now made home, leading to much discussion in the early part of the century that was, as Thomas N. Brown observes, "devoted to justifying immigrant loyalty to Ireland and reconciling it with their loyalty to the United States."[77]

The Church and Americanization

The many devout Catholics among Irish Americans were encouraged by the church's American leadership to integrate into American society. Historian Thomas J. Rowland notes this, writing, "If, in the nineteenth century, Catholicism had proven to be the outstanding obstruction to acceptance into American society, it had by 1914 become the most active and useful agent in promoting integration."[78] One topic church leaders addressed was temperance. Several church leaders began to advocate temperance, primarily to counteract the stereotype of Irish Americans as unruly drunkards.

Catholic journalists also encouraged Irish Americans to assimilate and were, as one historian writes, "absorbed with reconciling their Catholic constituency with American political and social institutions. Essentially, they sought and demanded acceptance and respect."[79] Journalists began to write articles highlighting the adherence of Catholics to law and order; they also focused on other positive characteristics of Irish Catholics, painting them as honest, law-abiding American citizens. Catholic journalists also instructed parents among their readership on how to raise children to be responsible citizens.

An Irish American woman waves a flag from her window. Irish Americans have been so thoroughly assimilated into American culture that some of them worry that they have lost an important part of their identity.

As they worked to promote assimilation into American culture, Catholic clergy attempted to repress the more radical forms of Irish nationalism, such as Clan na Gael. Although not discouraging nationalism altogether, church leaders like Archbishop John Ireland wrote articles such as one in which he reminded readers that "America demands that all who live on her soil and are protected by her flag be Americans."[80]

With the encouragement and assistance of the Catholic Church and having fought bravely in several wars, by the 1920s Irish Americans had made great strides in gaining social acceptance. American participation in World War II, starting in 1941, again allowed the Irish Americans to reaffirm their loyalty to their country.

By the middle of the twentieth century, Irish Americans had overcome stereotypes and had been thoroughly accepted into American society. As they rejected the stereotypes, however, the Irish also turned away from most of what made them "Irish" in the first place. It was as though they had pulled so far away from their former identity that they, as writer Andrew Greeley notes, "overacculturated" and "stopped being Irish."[81] It was easier for them to blend into society, Greeley explains, because they already spoke the same language as most Americans and looked much like them. Lawrence J. McCaffrey agrees and explains

"Teeth You Only See in America"

Writer Frank McCourt was born in Brooklyn, New York, in 1930, but when he was four his Irish parents decided to return to Limerick, Ireland. After failing to hold down several jobs and spending all of his wages in saloons, his father deserted the family, leaving Frank, his mother, and his brothers to fend for themselves. They lived hand-to-mouth, living on scraps and handouts and wearing rags. When McCourt was a teenager, he worked until he was able to save enough money to return to America; he did so in 1949 at the age of nineteen. Because he left the United States at such a young age, nothing he found upon returning was familiar. In his book, *'Tis,* McCourt recalls how out of place he felt around the Americans of his age group who congregated in the Biltmore, a luxurious hotel where he had gotten a job cleaning the lobby:

> There are two waiters working in the lobby and they rush back and forth, running into each other and barking in Greek. They tell me, You, Irish, come 'ere, clean up, empty . . . ashtray, take garbage, come on, come on, less go, you drunk or sompin'? They yell at me in front of the college students who swarm in on Thursdays and Fridays. I wouldn't mind Greeks yelling at me if they didn't do it in front of the college girls who are golden. They toss their hair and smile with teeth you see only in America, white, perfect, and everyone has tanned movie star legs. The boys sport crew cuts, the teeth, football shoulders, and they're easy with the girls. . . . They might be my age but I move among them ashamed of my uniform and my dustpan and broom. I wish I could be invisible but I can't.

McCourt eventually went to college himself and became a high-school English teacher in New York City. His books about his experiences growing up in Ireland and returning to the United States have become best-sellers.

Brooklyn-born writer Frank McCourt has achieved fame with his books Angela's Ashes *and* 'Tis.

further that Irish Americans became "physically, linguistically, economically, and culturally indistinguishable from Anglo-Americans."[82] They had left the city neighborhoods and moved to the suburbs, took jobs as doctors and lawyers, and were accepted into the country clubs.

The Invisible Irish

By the 1960s the Irish in America had assimilated so thoroughly that they were becoming invisible—that is, their Irish ancestry was rarely cause for comment. Some Americans of Irish descent saw this as a kind of mixed blessing. The society the Irish so longed to be a part of required that they lose something of themselves. Greeley writes that Irish Americans "made it by forgetting their past and trying to be like everyone else; they successfully imitated much of the achievement and style of big-city Protestants. During the process, much of the poetry, the laughter, the mysticism, and the style of the Irish past was lost."[83]

During the first decades of the twentieth century, even those Irish Americans who achieved financial success were not always accepted into established society; as a result, they created an elite class of their own, whose wealthy members staged lavish parties and other social functions. As the century progressed, however, that practice died out, as Irish Americans were welcomed into the homes of the rest of upper-class America.

As they began to move among the American elite, wealthy Irish Americans became in some way less Irish than their forebears had been. As Frank McCourt, author of the book *Angela's Ashes,* states, "The Irish were ashamed of themselves when they got here. They dropped the O's and the Mc's from their names. They were so busy hanging on and then prospering and coming right up against the establishment they lost sight of themselves."[84]

An interviewer for an oral history project in Connecticut encountered a similar phenomenon. As he recalled the responses of the many Irish Americans he interviewed for the project, he noted, "I found that at the lower social class levels people frequently thought of themselves as Irish and talked about it comfortably. At the professional level, more people tended to think of themselves as lawyers, or teachers, or businessmen, or whatever, and being Irish was not of particular importance to them."[85] The move from the old Irish enclaves to suburbia seemed to provide what writer Marjorie R. Fallows calls a "social break with an Irish ethnic identity."[86]

The Loss of History

Another casualty of the desire of Irish Americans to blend in with their American neighbors was the loss of stories from the past, of a sense of history. The Irish are among the few American ethnic groups that have not passed down family histories. Although it is true that first-generation immigrants who came to America during the famine years could little forget their past, many tried to; for them, the past meant pain and hunger. As sociologist Reginald Byron observes, "The previous generations were not especially interested in where their ancestors had come from, or when, but rather in making lives for themselves and investing in the future through their children."[87] Second-generation Irish immigrants heard a story or two from their parents and grandparents about the savage famine years, but by the time their children were born, few stories were being told, and few had been written down. Even fewer later immigrants passed down stories of their homeland, instead concentrating on making their way in the United States. One Irish American interviewed during the 1990s said,

> My father was a policeman. He wasn't interested in his background. It wasn't important to him at all, and he didn't talk about it much. His people forgot about everything in Ireland because they knew they'd never go back there again, I suppose. People didn't go back. . . . My husband wasn't interested in his background, either. It wasn't the thing then. Everybody wanted to be American.[88]

Another person stated that, "[With] the passing of the older generation, my parents, the Irish identity, particularly from my father's side, slowly fades away, leaving only half-remembered stories of family events and history."[89]

A few historians believe this omission was a result of the way Irish Americans were raised. Historian Thomas O'Connor writes, "There seems to have been a strong element of humility and self-abnegation in the typical Irish-Catholic upbringing that discouraged individuals from feeling that they were important enough to record their own stories."[90]

The Loss of Community

Another loss suffered as Irish Americans blended into society was the cohesiveness that defined the idea of community. In part, this phenomenon was just part of a broader shift in America, brought on by the passage, after World War II, of the GI Bill, which provided money to veterans for their higher education. Irish American veterans took advantage of the bill, and Andrew Greeley declares that this opportunity to get a college education was a turning point for Irish Americans, who with college degrees, could then earn the money that would pay for homes in the rapidly growing suburbs.

But once the Irish began moving out of city neighborhoods, farther away from the churches in which they had been raised, the church-centered lifestyle that had been the foundation for many Irish American families disappeared. During the early 1990s one Irish American said that, "because of the flight to the suburbs, the parish is no longer the centre of family life."[91]

As they drifted away from the neighborhoods where their parents and grandparents had lived, the Irish Americans began to meet, and ultimately marry, people who were not of Irish heritage. And whereas it had once been unlikely that an Irish Catholic would marry outside the faith, now such unions were becoming more and more common.

The Loss of Culture

In part, the gradual loss of their cultural identity was the result of conscious decisions. As they struggled to overcome negative stereotypes, Irish Americans turned their backs on anything that they associated with those stereotypes, including Irish music and drama. As Greeley writes, it was "as though in the desperate quest for respectability, the American Irish overreacted and eliminated not only the unfavorable components of the stereotype but those that gave them a positive distinction."[92] Thomas J. Rowland says they had developed "an overly sensitive and defensive outlook"[93] when reviewing the de-

pictions of the Irish in print and on stage, an attitude that seemed, for a while, to limit their participation in anything Irish.

A Two-Way Street

The process of assimilation for Irish Americans was really a two-way street: As the Irish in America were struggling to conform to American society, American society was gradually adapting to them. Certain Irish

An Irish-Catholic President

For many Irish Americans, the true test of acceptance was finally passed when one of their own, an Irish Catholic from Boston named John F. Kennedy, was elected president of the United States in 1960. Kennedy differed from many Irish Americans in that he came from a wealthy home and was educated at the oldest and probably the most prestigious educational institution in the country, Harvard University. Kennedy's father, Joseph P. Kennedy, had become a multimillionaire through stock market investments as well as other business deals. He groomed his oldest son to go into politics, but when that son died during World War II, he turned to his second son, John, who became a senator and later the Democratic Party's nominee for president. Kevin Kenny writes in *The American Irish: A History* that Kennedy's election "was a historic turning point in the history of the American Irish, marking their final acceptance as

full Americans." Kennedy was not the first president of Irish descent—Andrew Jackson claims that role—but he was the first Irish American Catholic to serve as president. Other presidents had Irish ancestry as well, including Ulysses S. Grant, James Earl Carter, Ronald Reagan, and Bill Cinton.

John F. Kennedy was the first Irish American Catholic to be elected president of the United States.

traditions came to be adopted by Americans of other ancestry and so became a part of American popular culture. St. Patrick's Day in the United States, for example, has become a secular celebration, a time to go to a parade, wear green clothing, and play at being Irish.

Even more important, American society, which up until the middle of the nineteenth century had been dominated by people of British descent, was forced to accept the idea that the United States should be a home for ethnic groups other than their own. As Kevin Kenny writes, "The Irish presence in the United States had decisively altered the terms of the racial and cultural debate over the meaning of America."[94]

Longing for an Identity

As their collective memory of the famine years faded, Irish Americans began to look again toward their ancestral home. For them, Ireland was not a famine-ravaged land—many had not even heard stories about the Irish Famine. Instead, they viewed Ireland as a green paradise, a charming homeland with quaint cottages and mist-shrouded hills. As James Carroll writes, "Those who emigrated began thinking of Ireland as a mythic place, and their children and grandchildren learned to think of it as a kind of lost paradise. Blarney-struck American entertainers and politicians exploited the fantasy."[95] Thanks to America's filmmakers, Ireland became for a while in the minds of Americans a magical land, complete with leprechauns and rainbows, where people danced in the streets. As they turned their eyes toward this idealized land, Irish Americans began to long for their lost identity and to wonder where their forebears had come from, what kind of food they ate, and what kind of music they made.

Tracing Their Roots

One approach Irish Americans took in reclaiming their ethnic identity was researching their ancestry. Some even go to Ireland to do so and are surprised by the feelings they experience when they visit there and confront their past. One couple who went to Ireland to trace their roots says, "Not to get too religious about it, but it does feel like a religious experience because you are going back and making contacts with the past. . . . Instead of just seeing a mountain, it's a mountain that maybe somebody in your past has traversed."[96] Jane Duffin, editor of the Philadelphia newspaper *Irish Edition,* agrees with that sentiment, explaining that she did not realize that she had been raised with any sort of ethnic identity until she went to Ireland, where, she says, "I felt I was home. I felt as if everyone I saw was related to me. That we were from the same socioeconomic background, had the same values, the same norms and ways of addressing things."[97]

Irish American Culture

Along with the interest in their ancestry, Irish Americans have also begun exploring the culture of Ireland, particularly music and dancing. Classes in Irish dancing are offered all over the country. Irish musicians such as the Chieftans perform to sell-out

Irish dancer Michael Flatley performs in Zurich, Switzerland, in 2000. Many Irish Americans have turned to Flatley and other ambassadors of Irish culture to reconnect with their Irish heritage.

crowds, and their tapes and CDs sell in the millions. One Irish American, Larry Mc-Cullough, explains his interest in Irish music: "My family had become completely Americanized and assimilated, and I was looking for something more specific. . . . When I discovered Irish music, I said, 'This is mine, I belong here.'"[98]

For all the interest among Americans in all things Irish, some note that the culture brought to America by the Irish in the nineteenth century is gone forever. Former New York senator Daniel Patrick Moynihan, himself an Irish American, observes, "It is, or ought to be, clear that there is no possibility—not the most remote—that a distinctive Irish identity can be re-created in the United States." Moynihan goes on, "But there is no need for the recreation of a distinctive Irish identity. It is enough to hope that the Irish experience, as that of others, may become a part of the American sensibility."[99]

Sociologists agree, pointing out that Irish Americans cannot experience an Irish identity, but they can experience something else: an Irish American identity that has developed over time. For example, the music that the earliest Irish immigrants—those who came even before the famine immigrants and who settled in Appalachia—developed over the years into what is now called "roots" music, a form that is exclusively American. Irish novelists such as F. Scott Fitzgerald and James T. Farrell and playwrights like Eugene O'Neill wrote from a distinctly Irish American viewpoint, and writers such as Frank McCourt continue to uphold that tradition. The Irish themselves acknowledge the divergence between their culture and that of

Irish Americans. Sean O'Huiginn, Ireland's ambassador to the United States, says of the culture, "I think we need to be understanding that Irish America is a culture with its own entitlements."[100]

Today it seems that the descendants of the famine immigrants have almost completely blended into society. Yet not so long ago, people of Irish descent found themselves constantly having their American-ness questioned. Joseph P. Kennedy, whose son John would one day be elected president, once noted in frustration: "I was born here. My children were born here. What the hell do I have to do to be called an American?"[101] Kennedy lived to see his son elected, living proof that the Irish had truly been accepted as Americans.

EPILOGUE

The Future of Irish Americans

As the twenty-first century opened, much of what had once defined Irish Americans had vanished, replaced by other characteristics. One example of this shift is the changing relationship between Irish Americans, the Democratic Party, and the Catholic Church.

It was not much of an exaggeration to say that during most of the nineteenth and early twentieth centuries most Irish Catholics in America were Democrats, and most Irish Democrats were Catholic. By the dawn of the twenty-first century, however, that had changed. The Catholic Church and the Democratic Party, once central institutions in the lives of many Irish Americans, no longer played such significant roles in their lives.

Becoming Republicans

Irish Americans began moving away from the Democratic Party during the 1950s, just as they reached a level of prosperity that could be called "middle class." As they entered the upper echelons of business as owners and managers, Irish Americans gradually began gravitating toward the Republican Party.

In fact, when John F. Kennedy ran as a Democrat for president in 1960, many of his fellow Irish Americans did not vote for him. By rejecting an Irish Catholic for president, Irish Americans were exhibiting a level of confidence and independent behavior previously unknown to them. Whereas in the past Irish Americans had felt that they needed one of their own in office to protect their interests, now they realized that they could accomplish what they wanted to irrespective of their ethnicity. Although 78 percent of Irish Catholics voted for the Democratic presidential nominee, Lyndon B. Johnson, in 1964, in subsequent elections more and more voted Republican. In some measure this change reflects the growing wealth among Irish Americans, but the pro-abortion stance of Democratic candidates tends to alienate the still-largely Catholic Irish Americans.

Questioning the Church

Yet despite retaining some strongly Catholic values such as the opposition to abortion, as the twentieth century waned, Irish Americans also began to take a different view of the Catholic Church. It was no longer the center of their lives, and the leaders of the church did not necessarily have the final word in how Irish Americans lived their lives. In fact, as historian Lawrence J. McCaffrey states, "Irish Catholics, once 'the most docile and faithful' in the flock, now 'tend to be the most critical and rebellious.'"[102]

As Irish Americans began to question the church's authority, their attendance at church services dwindled. As a consequence, today only about 15 percent of the American Catholic Church's members are Irish Americans, although about one-third of the church's priests and one-half of its bishops are. The old city parishes that thrived during the late nineteenth century and the first half of the twentieth have dwindled or disappeared altogether. Writer James Carroll notes of this phenomenon, "No longer a

Former President Bill Clinton addresses a huge crowd during a 2000 visit to Belfast. A peaceful solution to the conflict in Northern Ireland was a top priority of the Clinton administration.

place to retreat to, it [the church] becomes a place from which to go."[103]

Influencing Foreign Policy

However their faith and political leanings may have changed over time, Irish Americans have been steadfast in their insistence that Ireland be prominently featured in American foreign policy. Prominent Irish Americans, such as Senator Edward Kennedy, pushed President Bill Clinton to make a priority of helping to broker a peaceful solution to the fighting in Northern Ireland. With Clinton's backing, a framework for peace, known as the Belfast Agreement, was finally hammered out in 1998.

In spite of such political achievements and their general success in gaining acceptance in mainstream American society, prejudice against Irish American Catholics has not entirely disappeared. Writer Calvin Trillin states that even the most tolerant New Yorkers, who consider themselves to be very open-minded, "take a sort of easement when it comes to the Irish," sneering at their "supposed conservatism, bigotry, and backwardness."[104] Anti-Catholicism, states another writer, Maureen Dezell, "is the anti-Semitism of the American intellectual classes, and much of that religious bias is rooted in historic Anglo-American fear and loathing of the Irish Catholics."[105]

Acknowledging Irish Contributions

Emigration from Ireland continued during the twentieth century, but by the 1990s the number of emigrants dwindled as Irish citizens realized they could get good jobs in their native country. In fact, the Irish economy boomed and American companies invested heavily in Ireland, particularly in the high-tech sector of the economy. In a speech that President Bill Clinton made when he visited Ireland in 2000, he said of these American investments, "I believe America has, in some tiny way, repaid this nation and its people for the massive gifts that your people have given us over so many years going back to our beginnings."[106]

NOTES

Introduction: From Desperation to Assimilation

1. Michael Coffey, ed., *The Irish in America.* New York: Hyperion, 1997, p. 69.
2. Quoted in Coffey, *The Irish in America,* p. 172.
3. Quoted in Mark Wyman, *Immigrants in the Valley: Irish, Germans, and Americans in the Upper Mississippi Country, 1830–1860.* Chicago: Nelson-Hall, 1984, p. 39.

Chapter One: Leaving Ireland

4. Quoted in *Illustrated London News,* "Ireland and the Irish," August 12, 1843. http://vassun.vassar.edu.
5. Quoted in *Illustrated London News,* "Ireland and the Irish."
6. Quoted in *Illustrated London News,* "The Potato Disease," October 18, 1845. http://vassun.vassar.edu.
7. Quoted in *Illustrated London News,* "The Potato Disease."
8. Quoted in Wyman, *Immigrants in the Valley,* p. 19.
9. *Cork Examiner,* "General Distress—Public Meetings," September 4, 1846. http://vassun.vassar.edu.
10. *Cork Examiner,* "Further Food Outrages," September 25, 1846. http://vassun.vassar.edu.
11. Quoted in Terry Coleman, *Going to America.* Garden City, NY: Anchor/Doubleday, 1973, p. 18.
12. Quoted in *Illustrated London News,* "Condition of Ireland: Illustrations of the New Poor Law," December 29, 1849. http://vassun.vassar.edu.
13. Quoted in *Illustrated London News,* "Condition of Ireland."
14. *Cork Examiner,* "Destitution in Cove," March 19, 1847. http://vassun.vassar.edu.
15. *Cork Examiner,* "Remission of Rents," November 27, 1847. http://vassun.vassar.edu.
16. *An Phoblacht Republican News,* "An Droch Shoal—the Irish Holocaust: Starving for Relief," August 21, 1997. www.irlnet.com.
17. *Cork Examiner,* "Death by Starvation," October 30, 1846. http://vassun.vassar.edu.
18. Quoted in Coleman, *Going to America,* p. 22.

Chapter Two: Sailing to America

19. Quoted in Coleman, *Going to America,* p. 54.
20. Robert Whyte, *The Ocean Plague: The Diary of a Cabin Passenger, 1847.* www.people.virginia.edu.
21. Quoted in Coleman, *Going to America,* p. 76.
22. Quoted in Edward Laxton, *The Famine Ships: The Irish Exodus to America.* New York: Henry Holt, 1996, p. 193.
23. Quoted in Coleman, *Going to America,* p. 99.
24. Quoted in Laxton, *The Famine Ships,* p. 113.
25. Quoted in Wyman, *Immigrants in the Valley,* p. 46.

26. Quoted in Laxton, *The Famine Ships,* p. 194.
27. Quoted in Laxton, *The Famine Ships,* p. 194.
28. Quoted in Laxton, *The Famine Ships,* p. 199.
29. Whyte, *The Ocean Plague,* p. 22.
30. Quoted in *Cork Examiner,* "Sufferings of Emigrants in New York," May 19, 1847. http://vassun.vassar.edu.
31. Quoted in Laxton, *The Famine Ships,* p. 165.

Chapter Three: Making a Home

32. Quoted in Wyman, *Immigrants in the Valley,* p. 48.
33. Robert Ernst, *Immigrant Life in New York City, 1825–1863.* New York: King's Crown, 1949.
34. Quoted in Coleman, *Going to America,* p. 201.
35. Quoted in Coleman, *Going to America,* p. 174.
36. Oscar Handlin, *Boston's Immigrants, 1790–1880: A Study in Acculturation.* Cambridge, MA: Belknap Press of Harvard University Press, 1991, p. 88.
37. Quoted in Handlin, *Boston's Immigrants, 1790–1880,* p. 113.
38. Andrew M. Greeley, *That Most Distressful Nation: The Taming of the American Irish.* Chicago: Quadrangle Books, 1972, p. 87.
39. Lawrence J. McCaffrey, *The Irish Diaspora in America.* Bloomington: Indiana University Press, 1997, p. 71.
40. Quoted in Coleman, *Going to America,* p. 29.
41. Handlin, *Boston's Immigrants, 1790–1880,* p. 76.

Chapter Four: Working

42. Quoted in Coffey, *The Irish in America,* p. 136.
43. Terry Pepper, "The Wabash and Erie Canal Through Huntington County, Indiana," www.terrypepper.com.
44. Quoted in Ronald Takaki, *A Different Mirror: A History of Multicultural America.* Boston: Little, Brown, 1993, p. 147.
45. Carl Wittke, *The Irish in America,* New York: Russell & Russell, 1970, p. 37.
46. Quoted in Wyman, *Immigrants in the Valley,* p. 102.
47. Quoted in Coffey, *The Irish in America,* p. 146.
48. Kenny, *The American Irish,* p. 63.
49. Quoted in Ronald Takaki, *A Larger Memory: The History of Our Diversity, with Voices.* New York: Little, Brown, 1998, p. 7.
50. Quoted in Takaki, *A Different Mirror,* p. 39.
51. Handlin, *Boston's Immigrants, 1790–1880,* p. 74.
52. Quoted in Takaki, *A Different Mirror,* p. 158.
53. Quoted in Ann Kathleen Bradley, *History of the Irish in America.* Edison, NJ: Chartwell Books, 1996, p. 48.
54. Quoted in Laxton, *The Famine Ships,* p. 166.
55. Quoted in Wyman, *Immigrants in the Valley,* p. 42.
56. Kevin Kenny, *The American Irish: A History.* New York: Pearson Education Limited, 2000, p. 65.
57. Kenny, *The American Irish,* p. 157.
58. Kenny, *The American Irish,* p. 150.

Chapter Five: The Irish and Politics

59. Handlin, *Boston's Immigrants, 1790–1880,* p. 131.
60. Quoted in Handlin, *Boston's Immigrants, 1790–1880,* p. 176.
61. Thomas N. Brown, *Irish-American Nationalism.* New York: J.B. Lippincott, 1966, p. 43.
62. Handlin, *Boston's Immigrants, 1790–1880,* p. 210.
63. Bradley, *History of the Irish in America,* p. 106.
64. Kenny, *The American Irish,* p. 113.
65. Marjorie R. Fallows, *Irish Americans: Identity and Assimilation.* Englewood Cliffs, NJ: Prentice-Hall, 1979, p. 113.
66. Bradley, *History of the Irish in America,* p. 115.
67. Quoted in Fallows, *Irish Americans,* p. 119.
68. Matthew Fry Jacobson, *Special Sorrows: The Diasporic Imagination of Irish, Polish, and Jewish Immigrants in the United States.* Cambridge, MA: Harvard University Press, 1995, p. 22.
69. Wittke, *The Irish in America,* p. 161.
70. Brown, *Irish-American Nationalism,* p. 79.
71. Quoted in Jacobson, *Special Sorrows,* p. 60.
72. Wittke, *The Irish in America,* p. 106.
73. Bradley, *History of the Irish in America,* p. 106.
74. John F. Kennedy, "Address of Senator John F. Kennedy to the Greater Houston Ministerial Association," September 12, 1960. www.cs.umb.edu.
75. Brown, *Irish-American Nationalism,* p. 180.

Chapter Six: Respectability and Assimilation

76. Quoted in Bradley, *History of the Irish in America,* p. 132.
77. Brown, *Irish-American Nationalism,* p. 28.
78. Thomas J. Rowland, "Irish-American Catholics and the Quest for Respectability in the Coming of the Great War, 1900–1917," *Journal of American Ethnic History,* Winter 1996.
79. Rowland, "Irish-American Catholics."
80. Rowland, "Irish-American Catholics."
81. Greeley, *That Most Distressful Nation,* p. 263.
82. McCaffrey, *The Irish Diaspora in America,* p. 4.
83. Greeley, *That Most Distressful Nation,* p. 126.
84. Quoted in Maureen Dezell, *Irish America: Coming into Clover—the Evolution of a People and a Culture.* New York: Doubleday, 2000, p. 85.
85. Quoted in Fallows, *Irish Americans,* p. 76.
86. Fallows, *Irish Americans,* p. 76.
87. Reginald Byron, *Irish America.* Oxford: Clarendon, 1999, p. 187.
88. Quoted in Byron, *Irish America,* p. 207.
89. Quoted in Byron, *Irish America,* p. 110.
90. Quoted in Dezell, *Irish America,* p. 73.
91. Quoted in Byron, *Irish America,* p. 195.
92. Greeley, *That Most Distressful Nation,* p. 27.
93. Rowland, "Irish-American Catholics."
94. Kenny, *The American Irish,* p. 261.
95. Quoted in Dezell, *Irish America,* p. 220.

96. Quoted in Lucrezia Cuen, "Roots, On-line." http://abcnews.go.com.
97. Quoted in Dezell, *Irish America,* p. 208.
98. Quoted in Coffey, *The Irish in America,* p. 84.
99. Quoted in Greeley, *That Most Distressful Nation,* p. xvi.
100. Quoted in Dezell, *Irish America,* p. 206.
101. Quoted in William V. Shannon, *The American Irish,* London, MacMillan, 1966, p. vii.

Epilogue: The Future of Irish Americans

102. Quoted in Dezell, *Irish America,* p. 165.
103. Quoted in Coffey, *The Irish in America,* p. 88.
104. Quoted in Dezell, *Irish America,* p. 145.
105. Dezell, *Irish America,* p. 145.
106. Quoted in Steven McCaffery, "Clinton Urges Politicians to 'Stay with It,'" *Irish News.* www.irishnews.com.

FOR FURTHER READING

Tony Allen, *The Irish Famine: The Birth of Irish America.* Chicago: Heinemann Library, 2001. Explains the background of the Irish people before the famine, then explains the impact of the famine on world history. Reviews the reasons for the bitterness between the Irish and the English. Lots of maps, drawings, and photographs.

Seamus Cavan, *The Irish-American Experience.* Brookfield, CT: Millbrook, 1993. Part of the Coming to America series, this book reviews the history of the Irish both in Ireland and Irish immigration to America. Includes maps and other artwork that highlight and explain the text.

Greg Nickles, *The Irish.* St. Catherines, Ontario: Crabtree, 2001. Describes the journey of Irish immigrants as they left their homeland and found their way in the United States and Canada. Includes first-person narratives of the immigrant experience.

Joseph P. O'Grady, *How the Irish Became Americans.* New York: Twayne, 1973. Explains how it felt for the Irish Americans to settle in a new country that did not welcome them and how, over time, they assimilated into the American society.

Megan O'Hara, *Irish Immigrants, 1840–1920.* Mankato, MN: Blue Earth Books, 2001. Describes what life was like for the Irish at the time of the famine, why they immigrated to America, what the voyage was like, and what they faced as they tried to make a home in the United States.

WORKS CONSULTED

Books

Ann Kathleen Bradley, *History of the Irish in America*. Edison, NJ: Chartwell Books, 1996. A comprehensive history of the Irish in America, beginning with emigration before the American Revolution and culminating with the assimilation of the Irish into American society. Includes many color photographs of Ireland as well as period photographs and drawings.

Thomas N. Brown, *Irish-American Nationalism*. New York: J.B. Lippincott, 1966. Describes the efforts of exiles and emigrants from Ireland to bring about change in Ireland.

Reginald Byron, *Irish America*. Oxford, UK: Clarendon, 1999. The author did an extensive study of Irish Americans in Albany, New York, and this is a report of his findings.

Nelson L. Callahan and William F. Hickey, *Irish Americans and Their Communities of Cleveland*. Cleveland: Cleveland State University, 2001. Provides a history of the Irish who settled in Cleveland, Ohio.

Michael Coffey, ed., *The Irish in America*. New York: Hyperion, 1997. Looks at the many experiences of the Irish in America. Includes essays from many well-known Irish American writers, such as Mary Higgins Clark and Pete Hamill. Photographs of modern Ireland as well as drawings and reproductions from days gone by add interest.

Terry Coleman, *Going to America*. Garden City, NY: Anchor/Doubleday, 1973. Describes in detail, with many first-person narratives, the struggles of Irish and English immigrants to the United States and Canada. Includes a great deal of information on the voyage experiences of the immigrants.

Maureen Dezell, *Irish America: Coming into Clover—the Evolution of a People and a Culture*. New York: Doubleday, 2000. An honest, up-to-date analysis of Irish Americans and their contributions to American society.

Robert Ernst, *Immigrant Life in New York City, 1825–1863*. New York: King's Crown, 1949. www.nycenet.edu. A readable account of the experiences of nineteenth-century immigrants to America and of their impact on American Societ.

Marjorie R. Fallows, *Irish Americans: Identity and Assimilation*. Englewood Cliffs, NJ: Prentice-Hall, 1979. Explores Irish Americans' process of assimilation and how it affects their ethnic identity.

Andrew M. Greeley, *That Most Distressful Nation: The Taming of the American Irish*. Chicago: Quadrangle Books, 1972. Traces the journey of Irish Catholics in America, with particular attention to Irish Americans after 1920.

Oscar Handlin, *Boston's Immigrants, 1790–1880: A Study in Acculturation*. Cambridge, MA: Belknap Press of Harvard University Press, 1991. The author traces the history of Irish immigrants in Boston and surrounding areas, explaining how the flood of immigrants who arrived during the 1840s and 1850s affected the social and economic structures of the city.

Matthew Fry Jacobson, *Special Sorrows: The Diasporic Imagination of Irish, Polish, and Jewish Immigrants in the United States.* Cambridge, MA: Harvard University Press, 1995. Describes how these immigrants contributed to the United States; shows the relationship of each group to its homeland.

Kevin Kenny, *The American Irish: A History.* New York: Pearson Education Limited, 2000. A detailed and scholarly study of the history of Irish immigration in America.

Dale T. Knobel, *Paddy and the Republic: Ethnicity and Nationality in Antebellum America.* Middletown, CT: Wesleyan University Press, 1986. Reviews the Irish in America prior to the Civil War and how other Americans saw them.

Edward Laxton, *The Famine Ships: The Irish Exodus to America.* New York: Henry Holt, 1996. Focuses on the famine emigrants who left Ireland during 1846 and 1851. Details the journeys of the immigrants, including excerpts from letters and diaries, and tells the story of particular individuals who came to America.

Lawrence J. McCaffrey, *The Irish Diaspora in America.* Bloomington: Indiana University Press, 1997. A thorough history of the Irish in America.

Frank McCourt, *'Tis.* New York: Scribner, 1999. In this autobiography, the novelist tells the story of his journey at age nineteen from Limerick, Ireland, to New York.

William V. Shannon, *The American Irish.* London: Macmillan, 1966. A review of the history of Irish immigrants in the United States.

Ronald Takaki, *A Different Mirror: A History of Multicultural America.* Boston: Little, Brown, 1993. Gives a nontraditional, historical view of multicultural America, including Irish Americans. Shows how racism and prejudice toward immigrants have affected the country.

Carl Wittke, *The Irish in America.* New York: Russell & Russell, 1970. Traces the history of every facet of Irish immigration to the United States up until the mid-twentieth century.

Mark Wyman, *Immigrants in the Valley: Irish, Germans, and Americans in the Upper Mississippi Country, 1830–1860.* Chicago: Nelson-Hall, 1984. Specifically covers the immigrants who settled in the Upper Mississippi Valley region; explains the work they did, such as canal digging and farming, and how they eventually blended into American life.

Internet Sources

An Phoblacht Republican News, "An Droch Shoal—the Irish Holocaust: Starving for Relief," August 21, 1997. www.irlnet.com.

Catholic Encyclopedia. "The Irish (in Countries Other than Ireland)." www. newadvent.org.

Cork Examiner, "Death by Starvation," October 30, 1846. http://vassun.vassar.edu.

———, "Destitution in Cove," March 19, 1847. http://vassun.vassar.edu.

———, "Further Food Outrages," September 25, 1846. http://vassun.vassar.edu.

———, "General Distress—Public Meetings," September 4, 1846. http://vassun.vassar.edu.

———, "The Landlord's Protective Garment," December 6, 1847. http://vassun.vassar.edu.

———, "Remission of Rents," November 27, 1847. http://vassun.vassar.edu.

———, "Skibbereen," January 6, 1847. http://vassun.vassar.edu.

———, "Sufferings of Emigrants in New York," May 19, 1847. http://vassun.vassar.edu.

Lucrezia Cuen, "Roots, Online." http://abcnews.go.com.

E. J. Dionne Jr., "There Is No 'Catholic Vote.' And Yet, It Matters," *Washington Post,* June 18, 2000. www.brook.edu.

"Gaelic: The Language of Ireland." http://members.aol.com/compgeek35/gaelic.htm.

Rosemary Gazzillo, "Nelly Bly, 1864–1922: The Best Reporter in America." www.library.csi.cuny.edu.

Hispania News, "Deserters or Unsung Heroes: St. Patrick's Battalion." www. hispanianews com.

Illustrated London News, "Condition of Ireland: Illustrations of the New Poor Law," December 29, 1849. http://vassun.vassar.edu.

———, "The Depopulation of Ireland," May 10, 1851. http://vassun.vassar.edu.

———, "Ireland and the Irish," August 12, 1843. http://vassun.vassar.edu.

———, "The Potato Disease," October 18, 1845. http://vassun.vassar.edu.

———, "The Tide of Emigration to the United States and to the British Colonies," July 16, 1850. http://vassun.vassar.edu.

Irish Times, "St. Patrick's Festival 2002." http://ireland.com.

John F. Kennedy, "Address of Senator John F. Kennedy to the Greater Houston Ministerial Association," September 12, 1960. www.cs.umb.edu.

"Mary Harris (Mother) Jones: c. 1837–1930: Who was 'Mother Jones'?" http://digital.library.upenn.edu.

Steven McCaffery, "Clinton Urges Politicians to 'Stay with It,'" *Irish News.* www.irishnews.com.

"Molly Maguires." www.spartacus.schoolnet.co.uk.

"Nelly Bly." www.pbs.org.

"Nelly Bly." www.spartacus.schoolnet.co.uk.

Albert Bigelow Paine, "Thomas Nast: His Period and Pictures." http://graphicwitness.org.

Terry Pepper, "The Wabash and Erie Canal Through Huntington County, Indiana." www.terrypepper.com.

Thomas J. Rowland, "Irish-American Catholics and the Quest for Respectability in the Coming of the Great War, 1900–1917," *Journal of American Ethnic History,* Winter 1996. http://galenet.galegroup.com.

Robert Whyte, *The Ocean Plague: The Diary of a Cabin Passenger, 1847.* www.people.virginia.edu.

Jerry Wilson, "St. Patrick's Day." http://wilstar.com.

Videotapes

Thomas Lennon, prod., *The Irish in America: Long Journey Home.* Burbank, CA: Buena Vista Entertainment, 1998. A four-part series that describes the journey of Irish immigrants to the United States. Includes four videotapes: "The Great Hunger," "All Across America," "Up from City Streets," and "Success."

INDEX

PICTURE CREDITS

Cover photo: ©Ted Spiegel/CORBIS
© Associated, AP, 84
© Associated Press, Jeanie Johnston, 35
© Bettmann/CORBIS, 42, 54, 56, 71
© CORBIS, 21, 29, 45, 48, 64
© Hulton/Archive by Getty Images, 17, 19, 22, 30, 58, 68, 76, 77
© Kelly-Mooney Photography/CORBIS, 81
Library of Congress, 70, 87
© Museum of the City of New York/CORBIS, 39
North Wind Picture Archives, 9, 18, 27, 31, 41, 46, 61
© Reuters New Media, Inc./CORBIS, 89, 92
© Sean Sexton Collection/CORBIS, 14, 75
© Paul A. Souders/CORBIS, 15
© Ted Spiegel/CORBIS, 83
© Underwood & Underwood/CORBIS, 53

About the Author

Karen Price Hossell has written more than twenty-five books for children and young adults. She lives in Florida with her husband, David, and their cat and three dogs.